OFFENCE AND JUSTICE

BY
SIR PATRICK BIJOU

Copyright © 2020 Sir Patrick Bijou

All Rights Reserved.

In no way is it legal to reproduce, duplicate, or transmit any part of this document in either electronic means or in printed format. Recording of this publication is strictly prohibited and any storage of this document is not allowed unless with written permission from the publisher.
All rights reserved.

This is a work of fiction. Names, character, places and incidents are either the product of the author's imagination or are used fictitiously, and any resemblance to actual persons, living or dead, business establishments, events or locales is entirely coincidental."

TABLE OF CONTENTS

CHAPTER ONE	1
CHAPTER TWO	15
CHAPTER THREE	55
CHAPTER FOUR	84
CHAPTER FIVE	100
CHAPTER SIX	133
CHAPTER SEVEN	151
CHAPTER EIGHT	200
EPILOGUE	216
ABOUT THE AUTHOR	221

CHAPTER ONE

The jury came back, half of them looking at the defendant and the other half looking away. It had been a tough case. I should know. I'm Patrick Sullivan, assistant district attorney for Van Patten County. I had prosecuted Leroy Johnson for assault. He was a hard-working man, a good father, and until recently a loving husband, none of which helped my case. But for some bad luck, Leroy and I might never have met. I sometimes wonder how my life would have gone if that had happened.

Leroy worked for Best, Marks and O'Reily, a good size contracting firm. He was a union carpenter, known for the quality of his work, and the 110% effort he gave. He worked sixty hours a week to support his family: a wife and two kids. He was a dark-skinned black man on the small side, about 5'6", but strong from the work he did.

On the Friday before Labor Day, the union decided it was time to strike over the painting subcontractor's non-union status. It was just one of those things. The general contractor had no choice but to go with a non-union firm, and the union couldn't let it pass. So by mutual agreement they quit early on that Friday. Everyone knew it in advance. They just failed to inform Mrs. Johnson.

Arriving home some four hours early, Leroy discovered his wife in bed with another man. Leroy might still have avoided a messy trial had the interloper just done the decent thing and left quietly when Leroy told him to get out. The six-foot four-inch 260-pound white man decided to contest his right to be in Leroy's home fucking his wife. Unfortunately for him, two times a week in the gym was no-match for six days a week of hard physical labor and an incensed husband. The first powerful blow from Leroy's right arm put the bigger man down. Leroy having lost all control at this point began kicking the shit out of his opponent. Concerned that her husband would maim or kill her lover and end up in jail, Mrs. Johnson tried to intervene. As she tried to pull her husband away, Leroy gave her a hard shove sending her careening against the thick headboard of their dishonored marital bed. She hit hard and received a mild concussion.

The case against Leroy was all about the injury to his wife. The assault on the larger man was a hopeless cause, no jury was going to convict Leroy of defending himself in his own home against the assault by the much bigger man. However, the laws on domestic violence are such that Leroy could not completely escape the consequences of the injury to his unfaithful wife. Nevertheless, few juries were likely to convict in the circumstances.

That is where I came in. My boss Stan Kondos wanted to run for the Supreme Court (oddly the lower Court in

SIR PATRICK BIJOU

New York where the Court of Appeals is the highest Court). He needed to appear tough on crime and to be a firm prosecutor of domestic violence. His problem was simply that he was as useless in a court room as any attorney could be. I owed my position in his office to the fact that Stan needed all the trial help he could get. Stan had assigned the Leroy Johnson case to me with the simple admonition that I get some conviction and he didn't care to what.

For the Leroy Johnson trial I pulled out my A game and played my cards perfectly. It would have been easy to make Leroy the bad guy but that was not going to fly. All three of his bosses came in to say what a good man he was. When Leroy testified, he told what happened just the way it went down without trying to make himself look better than he was. I had to work around the obvious fact that his actions were the result of extreme provocation. It was a tough trial. When the Foreman of the jury rose to read the verdict, it was anybody's guess.

"On the first count of the indictment, Assault in the First Degree... how do you find?"

"Not Guilty"

"On the second count of the indictment, Assault in the Second Degree... how do you find?"

"Not Guilty"

OFFENCE AND JUSTICE

"On the third count of the indictment, Assault in the Third Degree... how do you find?"

"Guilty"

Assault in the third degree is a misdemeanor with a maximum penalty of one year. I could not see Judge Anthony Drego giving anything other than probation in these circumstances especially since Leroy had a family to support, but sentencing would come on another day. Right then Stan Kondos, the DA of Van Patten County had his conviction which was all I needed. I was happy the verdict had not come in with the more severe counts, I would have felt guilty if it had.

It was after seven when I left the Courthouse. I was due to attend the Christmas party being held by my wife's firm. It had officially started at 6 p.m. If I hurried, I could get to the west side of Albany where the party was being held in just under half an hour. I would be late but hopefully, not so late that Laura would be upset. Laura and I have been married for almost five years. She is almost six years older then I and much more successful. As a financial lawyer, specializing in bonds, at the second largest law firm in New York, she makes more than three times what I do.

Laura is at the top of the legal totem pole. A Yale honors graduate she has been working for Brentwood & Stringer for seven years. It is how we met. I was in my second year at Brooklyn Law School when I interviewed for a summer job at her firm. She had come to the school to conduct interviews on behalf of Brentwood & Stringer. I was her last interview of the day. The placement office had specialized interview rooms. They were small eight by ten rooms with an under sized table with six to eight utilitarian chairs. As I entered the interview room; I was confronted by an exceedingly attractive young woman dressed in a dark pinstriped business suit. Her auburn hair fell to her shoulders and framed the white collar of her blouse which showed off her pretty neck. She had dark eyes and a smile that would melt an iceberg. She rose and extended her hand.

"Mr. Sullivan I am Laura Parker, thank you for coming." To this day I do not know what I said in response. I can only remember taking a deep breath and being somehow unable to let it out. I didn't believe in love at first sight, but I will not dispute that I was enraptured by my first sight of Laura.

The interview was a lost cause even before I was smitten by this beauty at a first glance. She asked all the standard questions. I had all the pat answers ready, even if I was mumbling my responses. This was supposed to be just practice. I was interviewing for a summer intern job at a Wall Street firm. The kind of firm that hired strictly from the Ivy League not places like Brooklyn Law. The interviews from the firm were a matter of courtesy. It was a kind of practice for both sides so that the interviewers and interviewees could both gain experience. The school got to say the big firms came and the big firms could say they looked at the local schools. It was a game that both sides played. Laura was getting experience asking the questions, and I was honing my skills at answering. Unfortunately, just being in her presence put my heart firmly in my throat.

At some point Laura began asking about Edward Kincade, the former secretary of Housing and Urban Development, the son of the late Nebraska Senator Arnold Kincade, and Debra Cassidy, whose father was the ambassador to England and as rich as they come.

"I see you are in Edward Kincade's class?" she asked.

"No, he is my mock trial coach. I don't take any classes with him."

Steven Fitzgerald (my oldest and best friend) and I were two thirds of an unbeatable mock trial team. The third member was whoever Ed Kincade decided to put on the team that week. Kincade loved to win and we were his winning duo. You could not say that Steve or I were great students, but we were fast on our feet in a court room and were the best. Kincade loved trials. He could critique every trial ever held and see the flaw in every prosecution and defense. He was a great observer and a great coach. But I always saw him as someone who could teach without being able to do it himself. I recalled when my father taught me to swim. I wasn't even four when Dad led me into the water and taught me to hold myself under all the way. Then he took me to the side of the pool and had me practice kicking my feet. When I mastered this, he moved to the arm strokes. Then he had me put it all together. By the time I was five I could laterally swim for miles. My father was the best teacher of beginning swimming to the uninitiated there was. He could teach anyone - but himself. A childhood incident that he never shared had left him with a phobia. He knew mentally how to swim, but he was unable to lift his feet off the bottom for more than a few seconds. Edward Kincade knew every trial trick that was ever used and taught me some that had not been used, but he never tried a case himself.

"They say he is going to run for Governor?" she asked.

"Don't know about that just know we face Harvard next week and Kincade says we are going to crush them," I replied. She went on about Kincade, talking and questioning me for a good hour. I didn't mind I was infatuated.

Somehow I'm not quite sure how it happened, we ended up going for drinks after the interview. It was the last interview of the day and lasted more than twice as long as I had expected. She just seemed to want to keep talking. I do not remember inviting her out but somehow I guess I did.

Anyway, that is how we met. We were married while I was still in law school. She simply refused to wait until I graduated, pointing out that she was working, earning good money and that we gained nothing by waiting. By then we were already sleeping together, and I was feeling obligated. I got a strong sense that she saw my wanting to wait as evidence that I was just using her which was not the case. I was deeply in love, but kind of afraid of the eternal commitment I perceived marriage to be. I was after all raised Catholic.

After I graduated, I followed her to Albany when she took the municipal bond position. Laura felt it offered the best opportunity for a partnership. The firm had seven offices. The Manhattan and Washington Offices were staffed by the cream of the Ivy League like Laura. But the smaller offices had less upscale competition. Laura had worked her way into municipal finance where the margins were small, but the numbers very large. A third of a multimillion dollar personal injury lawsuit sounds like a lot, but the expenses are huge and you handle a lot of losers for one winner. Bonds always pay off and while half a percent looks small you must realize that a billion dollars in bonds are involved. Millions can be made on each deal and the expenses are paper, ink and overpriced restaurant meals. There are other hidden, under the table costs, but those are never spoken of at least not in public.

Moving to Albany created a problem for me. There just were not that many jobs for a lawyer whose only skills involved trial techniques. The general public misunderstands about lawyers. They see the big name trial lawyers and don't realize that they are rarer then move stars. Only a very few make it and they need more luck then skill. Most lawyers make their living avoiding Courtrooms. I finally found a part-time assistant ADA job at Van Patten County. They needed a warm body to cover Night Court three nights a week.

Laura always worked long hours which meant my nights working were only a minor inconvenience. When Van Patten's chief trial attorney died suddenly, I was offered a full time job because by then it was clear that in a court room there were not many who could best me. It seemed for a while that things worked pretty well for Laura and I, but in the last year she has been making a special effort to achieve a partnership in her firm. I know that she feels that this year is do-or-die on the partnership. Her added incentive is that she wants to start a family. If she gets pregnant before she becomes a partner she may not get it, so she has been holding off until she is made a partner. At 32 her biological clock is starting to chime and not in a good way.

My part is to play the dutiful husband and attend every social and professional function and support her effort by relieving her of any domestic obligations when the baby arrives. I have tried to keep up my end on the social obligations as the dutiful spouse of a prospective partner but sometimes the ADA's job interferes. I don't always work the hours she does, but when there is a trial on I need to put everything else aside. Laura has tried to understand. We see very little of each other since I now have long hours during the day and still, catch Night Court once or twice a week, and she is determined to get her partnership.

It is always, "Just a little longer baby and we will have it all."

OFFENCE AND JUSTICE

I hurry to the restaurant where the party is being held. It is a big old place off Wolf Road called the Briar Patch, first opened about thirty years ago. They started the place by putting some used train cars together. Over the years they have just built and rebuilt the place into a kind of maze. There is a big central room with a long bar to one side and a series of rooms that lead off this like spokes from a wheel. I arrived just before eight. Entering I found the party in full swing. There appeared to be about a hundred of the firm staff, family, and friends all celebrating. Laura was nowhere to be found. I searched the crowd in the main room and then began to search the extensions. I was just about to give up and call her cell phone when I walked down a narrow lane of booths at the end of one of the rooms. It appeared empty, but I could see it reconnected to the main room at the opposite end. I was about to walk through when I heard her voice.

"Stop that someone will see." It was Laura, and her plea was followed by a giggly laugh.

I froze unable to move. My wife did not sound in distress, quite the contrary.

"Come on Laura there is no one back here. You know you want me as much as I want you." It was a man's voice, a deep baritone.

"Please I am married Frank, my husband could come at any minute what would he say if he saw your hand up my dress?"

SIR PATRICK BIJOU

"He's not here and wouldn't do anything if he was."

I began to move forward then, but her next words stopped me.

"I know that he isn't the successful and distinguished man you are, but I don't want to hurt him."

They were in the booth right in front of me, but I stopped. What did this mean? Did she want this man more than me? I slid into the booth one shy of theirs and pressed myself into the back.

"You want to be a partner that means making decisions that sometimes hurt others, but it comes with the territory. Besides he has all the benefits of being married to a successful woman. You're entitled to the benefits of being successful," he said.

"I know, but I'm not sure that Pat will accept the kind of arrangement you are suggesting," she said.

"So what can he do about it, he won't leave his meal ticket," he said

Laura laughed, "You don't know Pat. He will never let money stand in his way, he just doesn't think in dollars and cents."

"Look you have me on the string, if not tonight then when and where?"

There was a long pause then she said almost too quietly for me to hear.

"Wednesday, your place I guess. I'll tell him I have to work late, but I will still have to be home by eleven. Ok?"

Then I hear what could only be a long lingering kiss.

"Now let's go," she said.

"Wednesday," he said in a demanding tone. Then they got up and headed back to the main room.

I sat there transfixed not knowing what I should do. Had I heard my wife being intimate with another man? Did she actually make a date with him? Laura and I never had an actually equal relationship. I suspect in every marriage there is what could be called a dominant member. I don't mean that in some kinky sexual sense. Laura was a few years older, six in fact. She had a better paying job. It paid more than three times what I made and had substantial room for advancement. The best I could hope for was a chief deputy job that might pay me three quarters of what she was already earning. Nothing was ever said out loud, but she was the head of our household. She picked the house and drove the new BMW. It was only in the bedroom that we were a couple. The sex was, I believed, good for both of us. I could not imagine it being better, but then she was the only one I had ever been with and I knew the reverse was not true. I had never asked how many had come before and she had never offered. I had always assumed that we were now faithful to each other. Now I knew that assumption was either just wrong or about to be tested on Laura's part.

I got out of the booth and walked back through the restaurant the way I came. When I reached the main room, I had no trouble finding Laura she was standing next to a tall good looking man. I would say he was about six three a good two inches taller than I. He was older. I would say forty plus or so giving him at least fifteen years on me. He was just a bit out of shape; some spread in the middle, but not fat. Anyway the expensively tailored suit hid most of that and there was no denying he was the kind of man that women are drawn to.

Laura introduced me to Frank Patterson, the new head of the municipal finance group at the firm, the section where Laura did most of her work. She was just beaming as she stood with her boss. Frank gave me a smug smile that left me in little doubt of what he thought of me. We made small talk about the trial I had just completed and the victory I had. Laura was singing my praises as a trial lawyer. Frank, I could see was unimpressed. I wanted to knock the smug smile off his face. I knew I could take this guy, put him down good. He was soft. I thought of Leroy Johnson. What was the difference between us? That of course was easy, he was an honest carpenter. I was a heartless ADA, and I would find a better way to deal with my problem.

Laura soon separated us and began leading me around in what is the necessary glad handing of her peers and betters at the firm. These parties are more about office politics then a pleasant time. Laura was pushing for her junior partnership and that was essentially why I was here. It did occur to me that part of Frank's appeal was his position in the firm, and what he could do for one aspiring to junior partner. Eventually we worked our way around to Saul Solomon and his wife, Martha. I was by then not the least bit interested or in anything like a social mood. Laura didn't notice. Martha Solomon did, asking me if anything was wrong. I assured her that nothing was and put my best smile on my face. I did not need her saying anything to her husband. The firm was generally just referred to as Brentwood and Stringer, but there were actually seven names in the title one of which was Saul Solomon's. Saul whose friends called him Sal was a lawyer, but I doubt he had practiced in years. He was probably the premier lobbyist in the State Capital. He is a rather short, friendly man whose obviously Jewish name and descent are belied by his dark complexion and his Hispanic features. Martha is taller than her husband, a big woman in all respects. She is as outgoing as her husband and just as genuinely friendly. I had liked them both from the first time we met.

CHAPTER TWO

Martha must have said something to Laura who decided that we should sit down and relax awhile.

She led me to a table and got us seated. June her secretary was there with her husband, Willie. As were another secretary and her boyfriend. We were making small talk for a while, the guys naturally falling into talk about sports. Laura soon excused herself to go chat up a few of her colleagues that we had missed. I used the opportunity to pump June for information about Laura's office generally and Frank Patterson in particular. He had arrived on the previous August from the firm's Buffalo office where he did commercial finance. He was a senior partner. I tried not to let the questions get too specific because I did not want to appear jealous or suspicious, but I got the sense that June was being equally cautious about what she said. We were dancing around the elephant in the room that we both knew something was happening between my wife and Frank Patterson.

The evening mercifully ended early and we drove home in my car since Laura had taken a cab to the party.

"You're awfully quiet my love," she said. When I didn't respond, she went on.

OFFENCE AND JUSTICE

"The trial got to you didn't it?"

"I guess. The more I think about it the more I see a man driven beyond his endurance trying to defend his home. Leroy Johnson was a good father and husband. He was the victim of an assault on his home and his person. He was an innocent man who walked in on a nightmare yet he was the one I prosecuted: the least guilty person in the room."

"Wow, you've got that little boy-scout conscience of yours up." She stopped to rub me on my arm and kiss me on the cheek.

"In the legal world thing are never black and white. You have to do things that sometimes make you feel uncomfortable, Don Quixote. It's all for the greater good," she said then added.

"But I love you boy-scout, promise never to lose that innocence of yours. I'll get you out of the Van Patten cesspool as soon as I have my partnership and a bun in the oven. Then you can spend all your time tilting at legal windmills. Trust me baby I will take care of you," she said resting her head on my shoulder.

I didn't reply. We got home without me reveling what else was bothering me. That the only difference between Leroy and I was that he had more guts than I did. We were both tired and settled into bed. I had trouble falling sleep but eventually the post-trial fatigue took over.

SIR PATRICK BIJOU

I woke Saturday morning to a warm wet feeling around my manhood. Through sleep filled eyes I saw my wife straddling my morning erection. She had tossed the covers off me, lifted the bottom of the granny nightgown she had worn to bed the previous evening, and slipped my morning wood between her legs.

"Morning sleepyhead," she said with a wicked smile on her pretty face.

"What brings this on?" I asked. She had done this before, but not since the first year of our marriage when there never seemed to be a wrong time for sex.

"Well I've a wonderful husband who though tired and burned out from trial escorted me around a boring office party. He smiled and played the good husband and even did a little politicking which is his worse talent, being both shy and introverted. So he deserves his most loving wife's attentions this morning." With that speech out of the way she lifted off her cotton gown revealing her extravagantly shaped body in all, its glory.

She rode me slow and easy making no rush of it. I lifted my hands to her tits cupping the tender flesh and then tweaking her aroused nipples. I used my abdominal muscles to pull my upper body up until I could suck a nipple into my mouth. I teased it with my tongue then bit down gently when I knew she was aroused. She likes her breasts treated rough, but not too rough. She moaned and tried to twist away, but I caught her in my arms. Holding her as my mouth moved back and forth between her breasts. She began to move faster on my cock. I am not fast to orgasm and after waking me from a dead sleep, she had a tremendous head start. Then without warning she climaxed. I felt her vagina muscles clamped around my prick and then continue to clinch and release. She melted into my arms as we collapsed back onto the bed. She went limp on my body and lay still upon my chest. We lay there, me savoring my erection buried inside her, her still coming down from her release. She lifted herself up onto her arms, and then crushed her lips to mine, her tongue invading and taking possession of my mouth.

"You were a very bad boy," she said as she began to wiggle and slide herself over my erection. Taking her time but purposely picking up the pace. She deliberately worked her internal muscles to maximize the feelings of her movements, griping me hard then letting go until I was ready to burst. Then she eased off smiling.

"Not just yet lover. I'm not finished yet," she said.

She let my arousal slide back then started up again bringing me to the edge and then drifting back. This woman knew me. She was far more experienced in bed than I would probably ever be and she had spent the time to learn my buttons, so she could work me as she pleased.

"Shall I let you come Sweety?" she said giving her low sardonic 'I'm in charge' laugh.

"Yes," I groaned.

SIR PATRICK BIJOU

"Ask nice."

"Yes, please, Laura."

"Please what Baby? Tell me what you want."

"Please let me come."

At that she picked up the pace moving up and down me like she was driving a fence post. Her right hand buried itself between her legs and she rubbed her self frantically. A minute later she let out a scream and then said, "COME, BABY! COME RIGHT NOW!"

I let go with an eruption that hurt it was so intense. We collapsed together, she laying in the crook of my left arm. We lay in a contented after-glow while she fell back to sleep. My body still trembling with the intensity of our love making. I lay pinned by her body easily able to move her off me but unwilling to do so. The sunlight is filtering in through the bedroom curtains became more intense as the morning sun rose higher in the sky. I turned to check the time. It was closing on nine. The black cat that Laura had fallen in love with as a kitten last year came wandering into the bedroom meowing for her breakfast.

"Going to have to wait for breakfast Midnight," I said, not an original name I know. Laura stirred then looking over me toward the cat.

"Morning kitten. Sorry but mommy was horny," she said. Midnight meowed in answer.

"You made an awful mess in me Patrick," she said.

"What! I made a mess what about you. I'm soaked." I don't know how other women are but when Laura comes there is a lot of fluid. She does not admit this. The discharge is allegedly all mine. But she, I, and the bed were all soaked, and there is no way it was just me.

She reached her hand down between her legs, brought it back up, and said, "Look that is you."

Making a pouty face she said, "Want to clean me up?"

"No."

"Yes!" she said and began to crawl up me until her labia covered my face. Well what can you do I began to lick our combined excretions off of her and to play mischievously with her. I licked from back at her ass cheeks to the front of her pubic lips watching her arousal start then without warning I grabbed her thighs pinning them with my arms and dove in hard on her clit. This was of course the point of the exercise; we had done it often. I do not particularly like the way I taste, but I love her flavor and by now I was fully aroused again. I held her as she screamed and wiggled trying playfully to get free and I kept at her hard till she came, soaking me heavily with her juices. When I released her, she jumped free of the bed then leaned down playfully to slap at my erection. She brought her face very close and just touched the tip of her tongue to my resurrected manhood before jumping back with a laugh.

"Hold on to that, I will need it later," she said as she headed for the bathroom. "Do me a favor and feed Midnight."

As I fed the cat I tried to remember the conversation from the night before, had I misunderstood it. Was it possible she was leading this Patterson guy on until she got her partnership without intending to put out for him? I wanted to ask and yet I was afraid to broach the subject. We had never been the jealous kind of couple. I had never worried about Laura being faithful. So how do I raise these concerns?

That night and Sunday, she jumped my bones again and again. I was still trying to find some way to ask what was going on. Then Monday she was home about eight o'clock, tired. We passed a quiet night. Tuesday I had Night Court in Tomkrill Town Court. It is a small fairly rural town at the North East Corner of the County. It is mostly traffic citations handled by the town attorney. Once a month they have a misdemeanor calendar. The usual, domestic disputes that got out of hand, petty thefts, bad check claims, and all manner of disputes that would have just gone away but for the State Police inserting themselves where they were not needed. It can be a busy night or over in an hour. Depends on the breaks. It was a slow night.

Laura had diner when I got home about ten. She made sloppy joes from a mix, and oven baked steak fries out of the freezer bag, with a mixed salad also from a bag. Nothing from scratch but these had become the staples of our life. Laura was never much of a cook and our mutual work commitments dictated how we lived. After diner she dragged me into the bedroom. We made love very slow and with quiet passion, me on top in the missionary position. When it was done she cuddled with me.

"Laura, are we alright?" I asked not knowing how to frame the question.

"Of course, I just needed you tonight. We are very close to the partnership. Once I have that, we are set. This time next year I could be very pregnant." As she said, the last sentence she moved closer to me and wrapped herself in my arms.

"Do you really need to be a partner?"

"Of course! The money will make everything easy for us. I've earned it," she said as she turned her head to me. "Pat, you are not jealous because it is me and not you?"

"No, concerned about losing us because of something that is just about money."

"Oh, baby. I'm not going to change. I will always love you. It is always going to be us, just hopefully more of us," she said placing my hand on her belly and kissing me hard and deep. And that is where we left it. There are times in the middle of a particularly dark and lonely night I wish that we had been truly honest with each other, but then the morning comes and reality returns and I know that what happened was meant to be.

Wednesday at 5 p.m., I was sitting in the back of the 39 Corporate Woods Parking Lot. The building was a style less rectangular box; it was where Brentwood & Stringer occupied all the second and most of the third floors. I was in one of the unmarked Ford sedan that the DA's investigative staff used. It was a simple matter to borrow it for an evening. I just had to fake an excuse like visiting a witness who I had interviewed over the phone that morning. Laura told me over breakfast that she had to work late and that I should not wait up as she would be very late. She left me with a passionate kiss and a protestation of her love.

I borrowed the unmarked car because I did not want Laura to recognize my car. I waited outside her office. I did not have to wait long. Laura and Frank exited the building just after five and got into a two seater late model silver gray Mercedes. I followed as best I could. Frank was a driver with a heavy foot on the gas. They drove to Volponie a rather nice if the pricey restaurant just north of the Latham traffic circle. They got there about five forty and I could not risk going in so I waited in the car. About seven thirty they exited. A brief kiss took place as he helped Laura into the Mercedes and then took off in a very slow and cautions manner. I found the change in driving habits odd but had little time to reflect on it as he soon pulled into the drive way of a side hall colonial in Loudenville, the plushiest of Albany's suburbs. The house had a detached garage but he pulled right up to the front door and they went in. The lights came on in the hall and then in a second floor room. I waited on the street for about forty five minutes I saw the light on the second floor dim but still I waited another hour to make sure. Finally, I just gave up and went home.

Arriving home I took a shower and prepared for bed. I had no illusion that I could sleep. My mind kept playing over images of Laura with another man. I did not cry and not because of any belief that men don't cry, but because I don't cry. It does not mean that the hurt is not there or the pain not as great. I had all the feeling of sorrow and loss that I expect every man would have in those circumstances. Before the night of the Leroy Johnson verdict I would have bet my life that Laura loved me and would never be unfaithful. I do not gamble because I am not good at it and Laura had certainly proved that a wise practice. I pondered the question of whether her actions were the result of a lack of love or a lack of respect and decided that it was both. At this point, I felt too much self-pity to contemplate what I would do and put that decision off until tomorrow.

Laura came in about midnight. I pretended to be asleep. The marriage was over, I saw no need for a confrontation at this time. As I lay there Laura bent over and kissed me tenderly on the forehead. Then undressed and headed for the bathroom. When she returned to our bed she was scrubbed clean and in a plain cotton nightdress. She climbed into bed and proceeded to snuggle against me. It made my skin crawl, but I gave no evidence that I was awake.

Thursday was a bright cold winter day. I barely slept and rose earlier than usual. I did not want to see Laura and left before she was awake. At work, I was called in to see Stan Kondos, the DA. Stan had only one ambition in life to sit with his ass firmly on a judicial bench. To this end, he was intent on running for one of a series of judicial openings.

In New York the judges of the lower State Courts are elected. Oddly this court is called the State Supreme Court with the highest state court called the Court of Appeals. So in New York cases start in the Supreme Court. Stan wanted to run for the Supreme Court. Unfortunately, he lacked the money to buy the support of the requisite county political chairman. Although elected, Judges rarely have to run, and a judicial convention takes place where the delegates chosen by the various party chairmen pick candidates to run unopposed. It is a source of income for the party chairman since the seats are sold. Discreetly of course but sold nevertheless -the only caveat was that the appropriate Bar Committee had to review and approve the candidates. Just to keep the Judges moderately Judicial and the system appearing honest.

My old coach had put a wrench in the works. As Laura had predicted he had run for governor and been handedly elected. Governor Kincade had forced through a Judicial Reform bill. He could not get Judges appointed as opposed to elected, but he did restructure the various judicial districts more fairly and forced a special election for more judges before a judicial convention could be called. The State Bar president then stepped forward with a special screening committee. Stan Kondos as a DA with a tough but fair reputation had a good shot if he could raise the money to run the standard campaign, about a hundred thousand dollars. With that kind of cash he could expect the law firms to pony up an amount equal or double that for the front runner. Stan had to be happy about my victory of Friday as it played well to the women's groups and the law and order crowd.

Stan's secretary showed me in and to a seat. Stan wasn't there but entered a moments latter giving me a pat on the back.

"Good job Pat. Always know I can count on you."

He needed to. In an office that arguably did significant trial work and that the voting public judged solely on the basis of its last trial; I was the only genuine trial talent he had. The chief assistant and the only one of us receiving a respectable attorney salary Dexter Eling was a hopeless cause in a court room, but he was a good administrator. Dexter ran the office efficiently. I had no grudge with Dexter. He was a good and fair administrator which was the extent of his talent and he knew it. Unfortunately

Dexter despised me. There could have been a lot of reasons including that some people just dislike others for no reason, but I was reasonably sure Dexter was jealous of my court room successes or probably more accurately embarrassed by his own lack of any. The balance of the full-time attorney staff was just Sheila Kneeler, from an old line Van Patten family, who did whatever Stan needed done at the moment- more his personal assistant than an attorney. There were rumors about the two of them, but then there are always rumors. For my money her awkward physicality and generally drab looks were against a sexual element to the relationship. She might be willing, but I doubted Stan was. The rest of the staff were part timers and happy to stay that way.

We had three part time attorneys who filled the greater balance of their time working in their private law offices. They covered the various courts and let me and theoretically Stan cover the big trials. Stan only showed on the slam dunks or when the Victory lap was due to be run.

"Pat, I have decided to go for the Judgeship."

"Good for you -YOUR HONOR congratulations."

Stan gave a good laugh at that.

"A bit premature, which brings me to why I wanted to see you. I am going to resign early to run. I know legally I don't have to, but to raise the money I will need to kiss some ass and well with the present ethics wind blowing I would hate to get stung."

It made sense in a way. If Stan called in the numerous favors he had earned in the job while still in it he could be charged with selling his office. If he were gone then the campaign money was simply given on expectation. Of course, he would need a way to still leverage his DA office. His next words let me know what was up.

"I am going to recommend Dexter for the interim job, he knows the office and can always get assistance from me if he needs it," he said.

It made sense. Dexter Eling would be his man in case anyone were to forget what favors had been done. Stan had paused as if reluctant to go forward. At that moment, I knew something unpleasant was coming.

"We are moving up Sheila Kneeler to chief assistant." He said.

If Dexter was nearly useless in a courtroom, Sheila was just plain useless. She was one of those attorneys who got through law school by memorizing the work and regurgitate the answers on cue. They end up taking the bar exam over and over until lightning strikes and they manage a pass. Appointing Sheila had only one advantage, her grandfather was a state assemblyman and daddy was the county executive. Stan was looking at me waiting for an explosion. None was coming. What really did I care; I had no expectations that I would get the nod even though I was the choice based solely on merit. It was Stan's next words that would eventually seal all our fates.

"That leaves an opening full time, I am going to hire Mary Ellen Seamon," he said which brought me straight up in my chair. She was straight out of law school. I had interviewed her for the part time position she now held and recommended against her when it became apparent that she lacked the temperament needed in a courtroom. She was a very young woman, about five feet tall with short brown hair. She looked about seventeen and acted about the same. In a courtroom she was someone that the most inept defense counsel could walk right over and often did. We had her working the easiest night and town courts and still had problems.

"Come on Stan that will leave us with just me to try a case," I said.

"Not exactly, there are still Mark and Tony." Mark Steele, half of the firm Steele and Steele which he ran with his father, was a solid lawyer, but he made his money in his own firm and held the part-time position solely for the state run health insurance. Tony Lorenzo was very slick, but a bit of a character who could handle a trial but preferred not to. Neither wanted to do any more DA work then necessary.

"What you are proposing is probably doubling my work load. Question is what do I get?" Stan made a long face before replying.

"Bottom line is I got nothing to give you right now. Maybe in a year or two things will open up if Dexter can win the election in November. I know Dex and I will be grateful," he said. I could see his worry at that moment. I could quit which would leave the office in the lurch. A few days ago I would have done exactly that, but that was before my loving wife betrayed me. I was going to need this job so all I could do was eat this for now, but inside something snapped. I had always played things straight; yet here I sat fucked by my wife and fucked in my job, and let's face it, looking at a dead end career. It was time to rethink things. I felt an odd sense of relief.

I smiled as I said, "Anything else boss?"

Stan gave me a funny rather distrustful look, "No that's it. Sorry Pat but I had to make some choices."

And all of them to your personal advantage, I thought. Well that is the way the world works.

Back in my office, I closed the door and sat in the one perk I had, a big old leather executive chair left over from some past administration. I inherited the chair from the man I replaced. Tommy Maitland died of a brain hemorrhage one day in court with no warning, he was dead in ten minutes. He was a good guy. Divorced when his wife decided she no longer wanted to be married to him, he had three kids. About a year after his death his wife remarried. It was obvious she was just looking for greener pastures. Well she found them and Tommy was dead at forty six.

Someone knocked on the door and then without waiting entered.

Katrina Gomez was a pretty girl. Short with long black hair and dark brown almost black eyes. She had the loveliest pearl white skin. The skin showed the influence of her Irish mother, the rest came I guessed from her Puerto Rican father. She was a recent addition to the clerical staff. She always had a smile and cheery disposition. One of those people who always goes around happy and wants everyone else to be as well.

"Sorry to bother you Mr. Sullivan. I am collecting for Bea's retirement present," she said. Beatrice Thruman was retiring at the year's end. Katrina as low person on the totem pole was collecting for a present.

"What's the damage," I asked.

A little shyly she said, "We are asking the attorneys for ten dollars apiece and the rest of the staff for five, but really five will do if you can spare it." I knew that she must have gotten quite a bit of grief from the cheap skates on the legal staff foremost of which was the soon to be interim DA Dexter Eling. I pulled my wallet and handed her a twenty.

"I'll give you change you want ten or fifteen."

"Keep it, and it'll makes up for the others," I said.

"Oh, thanks," she said smiling at me. Then she seemed to notice the dark office and I guess my darker disposition. "Something wrong Mr. Sullivan?"

"No, what could be wrong. I have a great job and a great life," I said with a lopsided grin at my own joke.

"Ok, well if there is anything I can do, let me know and thanks for the generous contribution, I know Bea will appreciate it."

She left closing the door, but it didn't latch. I had to get up to close it as it began to swing open. That is how I heard them. Katrina must have run into our office manager Marge Zuckerman just down the hall from my office.

"What's wrong with Pat; he seems so sad," Katrina asked Marge.

"Oh nothing, other than being passed over and expected to carry the whole load by himself, I mean the powers that be have really screwed him this time," Marge replied.

I didn't hear any more as they passed down the hall, but the conversation I heard was enough. The whole office knew or would know. I was now doubly pissed because I knew I looked weak because, in fact, I was weak. I was unable to stand up for myself on the job or at home. Another man was fucking my wife and I was doing nothing. I closed the door tight and might have just sat there stewing for a while had not fate intervened. My phone rang on the interoffice line.

"Sargent Brandt of the Sheriff's office is here to see you," Sally the secretary I shared with Mark, Tony, and Mary Ellen said.

Sargent Brandt was not someone I wanted to see at that moment. Jack Brandt was the father of Mary Lou Brandt who had been arrested for possession of a controlled substance, cocaine and over an ounce, therefore, a felony. In truth she had been in a car with four other young adults. One of which Larry Washington had two prior minor drug arrests. It was fairly obvious that the occupants had all been using, but poor Mary Lou had ended up holding the goods. Sargent Brandt was a man with an unimpeachable reputation and the hard earned respect of his colleagues. He was not a man to come begging for favors, but he was a father who loved his little girl so he would belittle himself if that would save her. Unfortunately, I had nothing to give him in the current situation. With Stan Kondos looking to run for judge, he was unlikely to permit any leniency to be shown to the daughter of a police officer. As Ed Brandt came in I was impressed by his imposing physical presence. At about six four and two hundred forty pounds, he had the physical presence of a John Wayne and the square oblong features of a Jimmy Stewart.

"Mr. Sullivan," he said holding out his hand and giving me a firm, but a gentle handshake, "I am pleased to meet you although I wish it was under different circumstances. You have quite the reputation as a prosecutor."

"I also wish we were meeting in different circumstances," I said.

There followed a good hour of unproductive discussion where he told me how his daughter was a good girl who made a single mistake. She was an honor student at the State University and planning on becoming a teacher. She was good at math, but not the best at picking friends. A shy somewhat nerdy girl, she had been easily led into trouble. Her mug shot in the file showed a not unattractive girl who might have been 15, but the record showed she was 19 and no longer a juvenile.

"I'll do anything I must to help my daughter. Tell me what to do Mr. Sullivan."

This near fifty year old hero with almost thirty years in the Sheriff's service was calling me mister, and debasing himself to help his daughter, who I could tell he loved more than anything on this earth. Frankly, I wanted to help him in the worst way, and to fuck Stan Kondos in the bargain, but I saw no way at that moment.

"All I can tell you to do is get Mary Lou into a treatment program. She may not need it but it can't hurt and will look good." Then I added and I did not know why but some instinct was beginning to take over. Some little thought that I could not actually visualize was moving in my brain. "I'll call you if anything more can be done. I promise you to look for a way out for her," I said.

"Thank You," he said rising and took my hand into both of his. I believe I saw the start of tears in the big man's eyes. I walked him all the way out. As I turned back from the front office door, I took a look around. For the first time, I contemplated that I was no longer going to just take it. Now was the time to strike, while it appeared I was helpless.

I spent the rest of the day trying to figure what the back of my mind knew that the front did not. I kept coming back to Frank Patterson, rich, arrogant, and ultimately weak of character. I knew this from just looking at him. I just needed the right leverage, and he would fold like the useless piece of crap he was.

The waitress came over, a short attractive brunette dressed in a short black skirt and a white blouse that looked like a man's ruffled dress shirt. She wore a green name tag that said TRINA in white letters, she looked familiar. It took me a minute to place her. She was one of the witnesses in the Roger Hamilton murder trial. Hamilton was accused of killing his pregnant wife in a fit of jealousy. It was a once in a decade trial with all the requisite publicity and media ballyhoo. Problem was that the Prosecution's case seemed unshakable. The Albany County DA's office was already taking their bows before the trial even opened. Hamilton had to go looking for counsel hard-up enough to accept his case. He found that in Steven Fitzpatrick, my best friend.

Steven and I were inseparable as kids growing up in a part of Brooklyn called Cobble Hill. It has no hill. It was used by George Washington for an artillery emplacement during the American Revolution, and when the British drove the rebels out they took out the hill literally; it is just a flat piece of ground now, south of Brooklyn Heights. We went through parochial school together ending up in Brooklyn Law School, walking distance from our home neighborhood. We were in mock trial together- an unbeatable team. I could not resist going to watch Steve in action at the Hamilton trial held in the adjoining county of Albany. Had I been prosecuting, Steven would never have gotten away with his shenanigans he got up to, and Hamilton who was as the saying goes "guilty as sin," would not have gotten acquitted. Lori Lafave was one of the shenanigans. A minor prosecution witness that Steven had flipped. The first time the unprepared Albany County prosecutors learned that fact was when she began to shoot holes in their case from the witness stand. It was the first of a series of blows that inevitably lead to a guilty man going free.

"Hello Lori," I said. The false waitress smile she was wearing slipped a bit and she looked at me hard. Recognition did not come to her.

SIR PATRICK BIJOU

"I was a spectator at the Hamilton trial." She now frowned a bit. But I smiled and said:

"Steven Fitzpatrick is an old friend." That brought back a smile to her face.

"He's a great guy," she said.

"Yes," I replied.

"What will you have?"

"The Brown Ale."

She nodded and moved off to fetch the drink. As I watched her go I felt my sprits begin to lift. She was the mother of three by two different men. She received child support for only one and worked three jobs to support her family. It was obvious how Steve got to her. When she brought the five dollar pint of brewhouse beer, I gave her a twenty and told her to keep the change. I was sitting in Brown's, a Troy Brew Pub that had expanded by opening a separate whiskey bar selling high-end liqueur.

I had been following Frank Patterson for about two weeks. Watching him dine and bed my wife, but also just following to get a feel for the man. Tonight was Thursday and he had come again to Brown's; this time I followed him in. He sat at a table with seven other men all professionally dressed. They were clearly some kind of club or networking group. They were just talking and laughing. Guys having a friendly social boys' night out.

About 8:30, Lori returned to see if I needed a refill. Frank and his friends were still shooting the shit and drinking. They were between their second and third rounds. I was still nursing my first beer.

"You find them interesting," she asked looking over to where I was looking.

"No just one of them."

"Mr. free hands and tight fists," she said.

"What?"

Nodding her head towards Frank she said, "He's always ready to cop a feel if a girl isn't careful, but he is the cheapest tipper of that group of tight wads."

"Well, let me make it up to you," I said handing her a fifty and ordering another beer. For the next six weeks with the exception of the Christmas holiday week, I made a habit of coming to Brown's each Tuesday, Wednesday, and Thursday. Except for Thursday, I just had a beer and left an outrageous tip. Lori and I became quite friendly. She would be ready when I was. Frank never missed a night with the boys who turned out to be a group of bankers, insurance agents, and lawyers, as I suspected a kind of club or network for professional men. Just a bunch of guys helping each other out, and as Lori had pointed out occasionally grabbing the waitress' ass.

SIR PATRICK BIJOU

I had been watching Frank drive home to Loudonville after his night with the guys. Always well within the speed limit, extra careful not to get stopped. The uninitiated think that one or two drinks will put you over the driving limit for Alcohol, but a big guy like Frank would need more than that and in a very short space of time. His carefulness when driving after drinking had something more to it then innocent caution, and very early on I was determined to find out.

The 30th of December had been Bea's last day. She had done her thirty years with the county, the last sixteen with the DA's office. The party was to start at 2 pm. Chuck Spenser, the junior investigator, pulled the short straw and would be holding the fort while the rest of the staff went to the party at Daisy Bakers, the longtime Troy watering hole in the former Christian Science reading room at the corner of State and Second Streets.

I was due to be there, but at the last minute, I appeared to get held up by a call from the State Police. It was a call I had prearranged as an excuse. An hour after the DA's staff left, I let Chuck go telling him to keep quiet about it, and I would cover since I was stuck here anyway. When I was sure he was gone, I locked up but left the lights on. Bea's desk was cleaned out but her terminal was still alive. The IT people would not remove her codes from the system until the following day. I searched around her desk, and sure enough, she left her password on a sticky note underneath the middle desk draw. I signed in as her and proceeded to access the state's criminal data base. If anyone checked, they would see

Bea's name on her last day. They would need to look her up in her Florida retirement home just to determine it was not her if she even remembered.

Searching the name Frank Patterson returned about twenty hits. It took about half an hour to find my Frank Patterson. I had to smile as I read his record. Four years ago an arrest for DUI (Driving under the influence) reduced to reckless driving with a fine. About Eighteen months later, another DWI (Driving While Intoxicated) reduced to DUI, a misdemeanor, but another suspended sentence. He lost his license for six months but got very lucky. That meant he had two strikes because the first offense would count as alcohol related even though reduced. I had him, all I had to do was find a way to reel him in. Three strikes is a mandatory felony.

"Sargent Brandt please come in," I said. I had called the man to discuss his daughter's case. I could see he was grim, but hopeful.

"Did you follow my advice and get your daughter into a treatment program?"

He nodded in response.

"Good, then I have some questions to ask you."

"Anything you want," he replied.

"You said that you would do anything to help your daughter did you mean it?"

He sat up clearly getting a little wary. But with only a little hesitation he said determinately "YES!"

"Good- tell me do you still work road patrol on occasion?"

"Yes, sometimes I fill in for someone who needs the time off."

"You know that strip of Van Patten County that lies between Rensselaer and Albany by the Green Island Bridge, a little strip of land?"

"Yea, about two-tenths of a mile along the highway."

"Well let's suppose a late model silver Mercedes was coming along with say a broken tail light and you were working that night, say a week from this Thursday, and stopped this car and smelled alcohol on the driver. An arrest would take place I suppose."

"Well, at least a sobriety test would be in order," he said looking both confused and intrigued.

"Yes, a test certainly, since the occupant could be a high powered attorney and everything would need to be by the book."

"I am not quite sure I see," he said.

OFFENCE AND JUSTICE

I picked up his daughters file. "Now your daughter's case seems like a slam dunk and no real reason to cut her any slack, but a lot of things happen in an office like this. Files get lost and when some ADA has been stupid enough to combine everything into a single case file that goes missing, well a case is just lost. Dismissed -subject to being expunged. I could easily see this file getting lost say a week from Friday."

Brandt looked at me hard. I could see it in his eyes, hope and a grim understanding that he was being asked to do something immoral, but legally unquestionable. The wrongdoing would all be on my part. Even if I was discovered, he would be untouchable-just doing his job. The driver would either pass the sobriety test or fail.

"Just a test or an arrest?" he asked.

"A test that is sure to be failed followed by an arrest. But no worries when the party gets to the town court the best defense attorney will be waiting and the worst ADA. Those as they say are the breaks."

Sargent Brant nodded his head. "I know I will be working road patrol on that particular Thursday probably with a very loyal partner. But what time if you have any idea hypothetically of course?"

"Oh I would say 9:30 pm through 11 pm would be sufficient." Then we shook hands on it and he parted.

The last piece was the one I dreaded the most. I hated to ask, but I didn't see any other choice. As I have, said Steven Fitzpatrick was my best friend. For our meeting Steven picked the Legislators' dining hall in the Empire State Plaza in Albany just outside the Justice Building. An odd place until you realize no one would be interested in us and the place seemed designed for private little luncheons. Steven without even being told knew that what I wanted needed to be private.

"How you been Pat?"

"Good, Steve and you?"

"Only as can be expected," he replied. It was an odd situation. Steven and I were closer then brothers, but very different. His wife Susan was a lot like Laura. Susan was thirty two to his twenty seven. She was very successful. Susan was the most beautiful woman I had ever met in person. She had film star looks and an aurora of sexuality that you could literally feel enveloped her. She was also promiscuous. For years she had been having affairs with a succession of men. All taller and more powerfully built then her husband. Steven was short about five seven and slim to the extent that he appeared almost fragile. This was a misconception because I knew him to be incredibly strong and to have the endurance and speed of a race horse. He was also the smartest and the best looking man you would ever hope to meet. Plus he seemed to have a sixth sense for things. Susan could never have hidden her affairs from him so she just flat out came out with it and apparently they had reached some accommodation that allowed her one discreet boyfriend at a time. Now I was about to ask his help screwing my cheating spouse and I had no doubt he would help me. He was not just my friend he was the ultimate defense lawyer. He had not a judgmental bone in his body. After I had explained what I wanted and why, Steven looked at me with sadness in his light blue eyes.

"You sure about this Pat? This is just not you. I understand the anger, but perhaps in a month or two this will just blow over, why throw your wife away like this. Laura is not Susan she will come back to you; no doubt overly contrite and determined to make it up to you. That's when you tell her you know and are prepared to forgive her if it doesn't happen again."

"Sorry no can do. Too much has happened. I can't live with it. We are very different you and I for all the things we have in common that is why we were such a good team. I know what I am asking is immoral and illegal as hell, but I do not see how it will miss," I said.

"That just it. I know I can live with it, the good Jesuits that taught us in high school and college drilled all the conscience out of me, but you were always the good guy, the white hat, how are you going to be able to live with this?" he asked.

"Simple. I just no longer care, something in me died when Laura fucked that creep. I want my own respect back, and I mean to have it."

Steven just nodded. The stage was set now just time to play my part.

"Mind if I sit down Frank?" I said. He didn't recognize the man he had been cuckolding, but I knew him. I had waited in the municipal lot just down the street for him to park his silver Mercedes as he did every Thursday about 7 pm. I was parked well in the back away from the light. I gave him a twenty minutes head start then I walked slowly out of the lot passing by his car, a nail punch in my left hand. One quick move and a small break appeared in his right tail light unnoticeable while the car lights were out, but it would stand out like a sore thumb when they were on, of course by then he would be behind the wheel and unable to see it.

"Pat Sullivan, you know Laura Parker's husband we met at the Brentwood and Stringer Christmas party."

"Oh of course." He was a bit nervous -well he had spent most of Monday fucking my wife. It was President's day. Laura said she had to work, but I had followed her to his house. This was just over a week after the big announcement. Laura had gotten the partnership. I suspect the two were having a bit of a celebration. Anyway she came home and tried to fuck me as well, but as I had been for the last several weeks, I was uninterested. If she suspected anything, she didn't say.

She was all promises of how good things were going to be, she just didn't known how right she was.

"What can I do for you Pat?" he asked with a smug smile on his face - perhaps he was remembering Monday. I had waited until all, but two of his drinking friends had left. Lori had been especially attentive that night and particularly careless of her ass which she dangled in Frank's face every chance she got. As a result he had three good drinks in him all doubles except the last which was a triple. As I sat down she brought two more a single for me and a triple for Frank.

"I need to speak to you privately," I said just loud enough for his companions to hear. Accommodating fellows that they were, they said their goodbyes leaving me alone with Frank.

"What can I do for you?" he asked.

"Well it is like this since you have been fucking my wife, I could use some help keeping things from becoming a bit of a scandal."

That took him back a bit, but scum bag that he is he tried to deny it.

"I assure you that you are quite mistaken," he said forcing me to pull out my iphone and read off the times and places they had been to together and show the pictures of them kissing and his hand on her ass; this brought him up sharp. He was truly caught with his hand up the skirt of my slut of a wife.

"What do you want?" he finally said.

"Nothing too much, a divorce, just a simple exit from the marriage, but knowing Laura she is not likely to go down without a fight unless she is persuaded. You think you can do that Frank get the tramp to just go away?" I said.

Frank took a long pull of his drink and gave me that smug smile of his. "Well I think that we can all benefit from keeping things as quite as possible, but this is a no fault state you don't need a reason to divorce."

"Yes, but yours is a big firm. You can make it difficult for me and Laura is quite stubborn. She will take some convincing."

So we sat there for a good half hour drinking with the good Lori seeing that the glasses were never empty while we discussed how to handle my wife and Frank's lover. Just before 10 p.m. we ended the discussion, the smug, confident Frank exiting. I followed him out when he got to his car at the municipal lot he hesitated. He fumbled with his keys, and I thought for a moment he might call for a cab, but he got into his Mercedes and headed out slow and careful. But with a broken tail light he was headed into the trap. I gave him a good half hour head start before I followed. When I crossed the bridge, I saw the flashing lights they had him out of the car and in the process of being handcuffed. I drove right on by.

I stopped at the Latham Diner just off the traffic circle. It was ten forty. My phone rang I could see it was Laura no doubt wondering where I was. I let it go to voice mail. I had a burger and fries and lots of coffee. Laura called about every twenty minutes. She was worried but clearly not hysterical yet. She had no doubt expected me home much earlier. I needed to be sober for the next part. Leaving the diner at about midnight full of food and caffeine, I got home before twelve thirty to an angry Laura sitting on the couch in the living room of our modest ranch house. The house she had picked where she expected to conceive her first child.

"Where have you been? You could have at least called or at the very least answered my calls."

I took a seat in the wing back chair that faced the couch and looked at her.

"I didn't call because it no longer matters," I said.

"What?" she was all confused. I didn't seem to be reacting with the contrite behavior she had expected. Her cell phone began to ring.

"You better get that," I said.

"It can wait. I need to know what is wrong with you. You have been acting strange for weeks. Come on Pat out with it. What is going on?"

"Answer your phone and you will know," I said.

Reluctantly she got up and got the phone. I could hear only her side of the conversation, but I could guess the other.

"Frank I can't talk now I will see you tomorrow."

"What? That is impossible." Her eyes widened and she looked at me.

"Never, he would never do that, even if he knew." Then her head bowed.

"I see. Ok let me talk to him, I will call you back."

She put down the phone and walked back to stand in front of me.

"Frank says you, know about us and that you set him up."

"Do I know that you're a cheating whore? Yes, I do. As to setting him up well I didn't force him to drink,-guess he just got unlucky."

Laura more or less collapsed onto the couch.

"I'm sorry. So sorry I just wanted to make things better for us."

"I don't give a damn what excuse you give; it is far too late."

"Pat, please don't go down this road, we can put things back together. You will see it didn't mean anything."

"Oh, but you are very wrong, it is going to mean everything. What exactly did Frank say?"

"He said to tell you yes, he will pay the two hundred thousand dollars."

"Good, that is his end. Glad to hear it."

"No! No! No! I won't let you. That is not you. You need to calm down. This is crazy."

I could only laugh at her. "What, didn't think you were worth that kind of money? Don't sell yourself short, you are one high-end whore."

She stiffened at the words, but she kept her voice calm and herself controlled. She was a good lawyer in a tight spot.

"Please don't do this. I know you won't be able to forgive yourself," she said arguing the best aspect of her case. Not her guilt but mine.

"Sorry, too late. Now we come to your end."

"My end?"

"Yes, Frank has agreed to his end and believe me he doesn't have much choice with two prior offenses. He is facing a mandatory felony even were he to escape prison he would lose his law license for at least a year or two. So Frank has no choice, which means if you want things to go smoothly you will agree to my proposal." I handed her the property settlement agreement I had spent the last week drawing up. As she read it over I saw her eyes go wide.

"Do you really hate me this much?"

"Yes."

She could do no more than shake her head. It was quite the agreement. I got everything. The house, her pension and all our savings, she got her BMW and five grand in cash and the clothing she wore. I even got the wedding rings. She just looked at me tears flowing down her cheeks. I had finally gotten through her defenses. I had won, but the victory did not feel good. I had the odd feeling that I had lost, but I pushed that behind me.

"Why, why, why are you doing this? I am so sorry. I never meant to hurt you. I certainly never meant to destroy the man I love. You will never get over doing this. I am not asking for myself. I love you. Don't hurt yourself because of something that is my fault. Please Pat stop before it is too late."

"It was too late the first time you spread your legs for him," I said, then I got up and left because I just could not stand it any longer.

Stan Kronkos was seated behind his desk. I had entered unannounced and without knocking.

Looking up he frowned and said, "What is it?"

I smiled and seated myself in the chair opposite his desk.

"Last night a prominent attorney was arrested for DWI, he blew a 2.2 on the breathalyzer, not surprising considering what he had to drink."

"So?"

"Well, it's like this. Mary Ellen did the arraignment and failed to get a blood test. She also failed to get a statement from the arresting office, Sargent Brandt, who will no doubt have a very poor memory this morning since somebody seems to have sheared the file of his daughter's drug arrest."

"What the fuck?"

"Exactly -what the fuck - or more precisely one hundred thousand dollars worth of fuck in campaign contributions from an untraceable source, all you have to do is go quietly off to run for Judge without recommending anyone as your successor and if anyone should ask, I am a very good candidate - an excellent choice."

"You're crazy. You will never get it."

"As I said one hundred thousand from an untraceable source."

Stan just sat there for a minute his mouth hanging open then he closed it and just nodded. I got up to leave as I made the door he said:

"You are the last person I ever would have believed capable of this."

"Well, you never can tell," I said.

Later that day I had a meeting with the Van Patten Democrat county political chairman, Tommy Lecour, in Malloy's restaurant where many political deals have been done.

"Well, Mr. Sullivan what can I do for you?"

"You can ask the Governor to appoint me acting DA when Stan Kondos resigns to run for judge."

"Any reason that I would have to do that?"

"I can think of one hundred thousand reasons and they are all green and have dollar signs printed on them."

"That's a lot of walking around money," he said.

The term walking around money comes from the cash given to ward captains on Election Day to cover incidental expenses. But it also refers to the discretionary funds available to the county party chairman. Money he can spend any way he pleases, no strings attached.

"Let's just say I have it and will make sure it is delivered by an unquestionable and unimpeachable source as soon as the governor appoints me."

Tommy though about it a minute and then extended his hand across the table. "I trust you are at least a Democrat, Mr. Sullivan?" he said.

"Please call me Pat and I am changing my registration this afternoon."

We both laughed.

CHAPTER THREE

New York is the largest city in the United States. It is one of the world's capital cities and home to the United Nations. But for reasons lost in the obscurity of Colonial American history, New York City is not the Capital of New York State. The State Capital is located in the northern Hudson River city of Albany, whose population, if deducted from that of the City of New York would still leave over eight million residents. The actual state government is operated from New York City or as it is normally referred to as "the City." The State's Capital is referred to as "Albany" a generic term that may refer to the city at the north end of the Hudson River or just the state government wherever it's located.

New York's Governors rarely spend their time in the actual capital city of Albany. The Governor's mansion provides neither comfort nor privacy. Albany itself sits in the south east quadrant of a snow belt that is unrivaled in North America east of the Rocky Mountains. While certainly not the coldest place in the state, Albany has both long and snow-filled winters and often snow-filled springs. As a rule, New York Governors spend as little time there as possible. Governor Edward Kincade is no exception to this rule, preferring his warm eight thousand square foot Central Park view apartment in "the City" to the cold climes of Albany. However, it was March, and as everyone in the New York State Government knows, the Governor must travel up the Hudson to Albany and pretend that the State Legislature is actively working on the State Budget. In fact, the Budget, due April first, will usually be passed in late June - in time for the July Fourth recess and the beginning of the election season.

Accordingly, this being the first Monday in March, Edward Kincade was in Albany. The Executive Chamber in the Capitol Building is known as the Redroom, which is used only for official and public events. The Governor's actual business is conducted in the smaller room behind the Executive office.

"Ok, Tony who's next?" Governor Kincade asked of his senior political aid Tony Greco. Tony was a man who prided himself on knowing everyone and their personal agendas.

"Tom LeCouer, our chairman for Van Patten County, he must be looking for money because they don't control anything up there. The republicans have the assembly man, the state senator, the county executive, and the county legislature."

"So Tom is looking for funding for the next election?"

"Almost certainly, but I don't see how we can spare it," Tony said.

Kincade thought a moment then said, "How about I offer to attend a fund-raiser or two for him? That should help and only cost us some time. I'm stuck here anyway."

The two men agreed and then the Governor's trusted Secretary, Mrs. Betty Morgan, showed the Democratic Chairman of the most Republican County in the State into the presence of the State's Democratic Governor.

After chatting a bit about Tommy's daughter's recent acceptance to medical school and his son's senior year at Doane Stuart, a high-ranking private school known for its great academics and abysmal sports programs, the men got down to business.

"Well Tom what can I do for you?" the Governor asked.

"Have you heard that Stan Kondos plans to resign as DA in order to run for Judge," Tom said.

This small tidbit of information was news to the Governor, but Tony quickly stepped into say that it had come to their attention that Stan was considering that move.

"Well, we are relatively sure it's a done deal and I would like to make the local parties position clear regarding who we feel should be the logical choice for an interim appointment." Tom said it a bit faster than he intended the words to come out, but he was a little nervous in such important company.

"I'm always happy to receive the recommendations of those as we say who represent 'the boots on the ground.' You are after all in a better position to assess local needs then I am," the Governor replied graciously. His words did not mean precisely what he had said. The actual translation would be that he had no one in mind and Tom should go ahead and make his choice known.

"Well, we in Van Patten County think the choice should go to the best candidate and one familiar with that office," Tom began what was a well-rehearsed presentation and now he had his nerves in check.

"I would not have it any other way," the governor replied, now wondering who is the democrat in a republican DA's office.

"We're recommending Patrick Sullivan. He is a bright young man and an excellent..."

Tony was about to jump in but the Governor's firm hand on Tony's knee told him to stay out of this and at the same time the governor interrupted Tom.

"You do not need to tell me about Pat Sullivan, I know him very well. He would make an excellent DA perhaps in a few years when he has a little more experience under his belt," the Governor said.

"Well he is chief trial counsel there right now and from what we know of the office as you point out governor, since we are 'the boots on the ground,' Sullivan is the only decent trial attorney they have in that office." Tom paused and then he said the words that stunned the Governor and his aide.

"Van Patten County believes this appointment to be very important to us," Tom looked the Governor directly in the eyes as he said this.

Edward Kincade did not think of himself as a highly skilled or even a natural politician. It was an occupation that he had more or less inherited. But at that moment nothing showed. His masterful political advisor Tony Greco's mouth fell open but Ed Kincade did not have so much as a stray eyelash to show his surprise. The words Tom LeCour had uttered were a form of insider code that meant that unless the Governor acceded to the request to appoint Sullivan, he could not count on Van Patten County supporting him in the next election.

Coming from the weakest chairman in the state, this was shocking. Kincade showed nothing, not the rage that he was sure his political advisor would have or the perplexity that he had. Edward Kincade knew Patrick Sullivan very well. He had taught him and he knew in a courtroom no one was better with one notable exception. The Governor knew enough to realize that there was something here he needed to know more about before he acted, something out of the ordinary, something that could either be trouble or exceptionally useful. Appointments could always come back to bite you in the ass. Ed Kincade was not about to make a blind appointment or lose a single vote by being timid.

"Well, I will have to give your view my full consideration and let you know as soon as I reach a decision," the Governor said. The meanings of his words were clear to those who knew the language. He had promised to do it if possible. Tom Lecour could ask for no more.

"Thank you Governor," he said and the meeting ended.

When Lecour had gone, Tony Greco said, "I'll have this Sullivan guy checked out right away."

"No Tony, you will stay clear of this," Kincade responded.

"But why?"

"Pat Sullivan's closest friend is Steven Fitzgerald."

The mention of that name brought Greco up sharp. Tony had been having an affair for more than a year with Susan Singleton, the wife of Steven Fitzgerald. The affair was known to the Governor. It was not a particularly well kept secret.

The Singletons were related to the deVoes, their mother was Kathern deVoe and their father, Joseph Singleton, the Insurance Tycoon. The deVoe-Singleton girls were known equally for their beauty and their promiscuity. Both daughters topped the ten most beautiful women in the world list and both were married to shy bookish men. Neither Susan nor Mary Singleton had ever, to the

Governor's knowledge, let a marriage ring interfere with a good affair.

Edward Kincade had never completely trusted Steven Fitzgerald. He was an exceptional presence in a courtroom, but there was just something about Steven that made the hair on the back of his neck stand up.

"Stay away Tony, no need for an unnecessary scandal."

Tony could only nod, he was in the awkward position of being hopelessly in love with a woman, who though she happy bedded him, refused to even discuss leaving her husband. A man Tony saw in every way as his inferior.

Two hours latter Don Pleasant, former NYC police lieutenant now retired, was meeting with the Governor. The Governor's official security was provided by the State Police, but Ed Kincade found it expedient to provide a certain level of private security for himself, for which he paid from his personal fortune. Don was the head of that security.

"I need you to find out what you can about Patrick Sullivan. I believe his wife works for the law firm Brentwood and Stringer. He is currently with the Van Patten County DA's office. The local Dems suddenly want to push him for higher office. Find out why and anything else you can. Oh and check the current status of Steven Fitzgerald. Don't let anyone know we are looking at Steven."

OFFENCE AND JUSTICE

"Gov, when do you need this?" Don asked.

"Yesterday, But be careful. I just have the feeling that something is off."

When Don left, Ed Kincade, Governor of the State of New York, clasped his fingers together and sat behind his big official desk and pondered how much things had changed since he coached the two exceptionally talented young men in the art of trial tactics. Were those young men now his supporters or his adversaries?

Laura

At least she wasn't crying. The last two weeks it seemed that was all she could do, but today the tears had stopped. It wasn't because it was a good day. It started off bad; Frank Patterson balled her out in front of the municipal bond staff over errors in the Corinth Bond prospectus. They were just typos. It was after all the draft prospectus and that is why it is a draft. Technically the prospectus is under her supervision; however, the real motive for her dressing down was something else. Everyone knew the real reason for Frank's anger was Patrick Sullivan, Laura's husband - soon if Pat gets his way, ex-husband.

You see Frank and she had what they viewed as a reasonably discreet affair. One where most of the office staff knew something was going on but couldn't say that things had crossed the line into infidelity. In public their behavior had been friendly and professional. A little flirting kept within acceptable bounds. The fact was that they had an affair with a considerable amount of sizzle. There was only one minor problem, actually more an inconvenient embarrassment than a problem. She was married.

Her husband was a shy introverted man -over five years her junior. A better husband could not be conceived. He was kind, considerate and loving, it was clear to all that Patrick Sullivan would walk-in front of a speeding train for his wife, Laura. He had put his career behind hers so that she could excel and she did make about four times the salary he did. If you took Patrick's salary away from Laura's, you would still have more than a hundred fifty thousand left over. But Patrick was the best of husbands for an ambitious career woman, he recognized she had the better career path and he deferred to her goals. In other words, Patrick was no Frank Patterson.

Frank was what is called an Alpha male. Strong, dominant, and possessed of all the words a woman needs to hear. Pat was something less, a kind of beta male; but Pat was possessed of something special. He had the qualities of goodness and generosity that Laura loved. He also had some areas in his quiet introverted personality that Laura had never seen, even after five years of marriage, there were aspects of her husband that she did not understand. They were a problem to her now.

OFFENCE AND JUSTICE

Laura met Pat when she was conducting interviews for her law firm, Brentwood and Stringer. It is the second largest firm in the state. There was little chance that Pat would be hired as a summer law clerk. Only, the best of the best, were considered and they were interviewed by the senior associates who would make the real recommendations.

Laura was one of the new kids. She was just starting her second year with the firm. She had taken the bar exam the previous year and passed. She was now admitted and gone through the tough first year were she worked eighty, ninety, and one week one hundred hours, all of which she billed to clients at $175.00 an hour. Now she was a full, if junior, associate and billing $210.00 an hour. She had come to Brooklyn Law to hone her interview skills. She had picked the candidates she was going to interview on the basis of their academic record and law review status.

Laura was interviewing only the top one percent and law review editors with one exception. The second year student, Patrick Sullivan's resume showed him at the class middle and no law review, but he did mock trial with Edward Kincade and had a personal recommendation from Kincade who many said would be the next governor.

Laura had a crush on Kincade. Not a Brad Pitt or in her case Liam Neeson kind of crush, but the Women's Bar Association kind of crush, where you admire someone that doesn't quite set your motor instantly running. Since Kincade was part-time faculty at Brooklyn, while he seemed to be traveling about the state building his political base, she figured that perhaps she could pump this interviewee about Kincade. It was the last interview of the day when a very young version of Liam walked in.

Patrick Sullivan was obviously Irish. He was tall with light hair with just a blush of red in it. But mostly she saw those deep warm sea blue eyes. She didn't normally notice a person's eyes first thing, but these were arresting. She was surprised when she discovered how shy he was. He was also several years younger than the average law student. He stumbled through the interview and she wondered how he could ever manage on the mock trial team. But there was no doubt she was smitten, at least enough to maneuver him into drinks after the interview.

Capulets on Montaque Street was the usual twenty something Brooklyn bar that no fashionable New Yorker would willingly be caught in. It wasn't terribly expensive, but managed to be just a little overpriced. It was completely tasteless, with Shakespeare quotes laminated on to the tables. The place had no style at all. The drinks were large and the food looked too fattening for any woman out of her teens to eat. They shared a pitcher of Sangria, the house drink that was oddly very good, but she quickly noticed that it had a big kick to it. As they drank, his accent came out. It was not quite Irish, nor was it a Brooklyn accent, at least none she had heard, although it sounded familiar. Sometimes she seemed to hear Dutch, but that might have been her imagination. It was clear and sweet and had a tone to it, reminiscent of a bell. But it was obvious that he did not know he had it. She was just about to ask him about it when his friends showed up.

The woman was a most incredible beauty. She was tall, maybe five foot ten, but not thin like a model, she had a striking shape with elegant curves as if she was the blue print for how a woman was supposed to be put together. She had big brown eyes and jet black hair. Her skin was fair with just a hint of a tan. Laura could not remember seeing any woman more arresting in the flesh. She wore skin tight black leather pants and a simple snow white blouse. She wore just the right amount of makeup and clearly knew that every head in the place turned when she entered. You almost did not notice the man with her-he was shorter maybe five-seven and looked much smaller because she was wearing four inch heels.

Steven Fitzgerald was easy to overlook, but once you noticed him you could not easily look away. He was the prettiest human being. He was a young Peter O'Toole. Like Patrick, he was shy but his light blue eyes caught Laura's and held hers, unable to look away, the second time that had happened to her that day. This is how she first met Steven Fitzgerald, whose nickname was Foxy, and Susan deVoe Singleton. As soon as Laura heard Susan's full name she knew she was the youngest daughter of Joseph Singleton and Katheryn deVoe. The deVoes were old money and Joe Singleton was in insurance or more precisely reinsurance. Brentwood and Stringer had done work for DeVoe Singleton, the third largest reinsurer in the nation and the largest that was privately held.

Susan proved to be one of those individuals whose personality is both unexpected and pleasurable. She was the ultimate extrovert who genuinely enjoyed people. Laura found herself falling completely under her spell. They talked and talked and found that they had much in common not the least of which was a driving ambition. The men were quietly sipping their wine and seeming to communicate almost without talking, when they did speak, the accent that they shared was even more easily heard, and it was obvious that they were both painfully shy. It was Susan who spoke for them telling Laura that they had grown up together a few blocks from where they were seated in the neighborhood know as Cobble Hill.

"Of course, it was not fashionable then. It was a kind of middle class ghetto caught between poverty on one end and wealth on the other," Susan explained. The boys were as close as brothers. They had attended the same parochial grade school, catholic high and Fordham University. Now they were in Brooklyn Law together in their second year. Susan had met Steven in a trendy Manhattan bar when the blind date his sister had set him up with, was as Susan put it, a little careless.

"I saw my opportunity and pounced," she said taking his hand in hers and smiling at him.

When Susan headed for the restroom she dragged Laura along. After they had taken a pee, Susan paused to touch up her hair and makeup.

"So how do you like Patrick?" she asked.

"He's well-I guess he is-sort of different," Laura replied.

"Of course, he's a virgin for one thing, they both are."

"Really? I mean they seem kind of innocent, but?"

"Yep, no doubt. I have been dating Steven since early summer but can't bring myself to just pop his cherry. He so sweet and frankly I got it bad for him. I am going to have to marry him, but he is so shy, I may have to do the asking or trick him into thinking he asked." They both laughed at this, but it actually was not that funny.

Dealing with Patrick proved to be quite difficult for Laura. She had to put her phone number on the back of her business card and make sure he had it in his pocket when they parted that evening. She of course had his number and his address from his resume, but she wanted him to call. Three days passed without a call from him. She got a call from Susan inviting her out the following weekend.

"Will Pat be there? He hasn't called me," she told Susan who laughed.

"Don't worry, he was crazy for you, he is just working up his nerve. I'll get Steven to push him."

The following day Pat called and they set up a double date for Saturday night. So it went with Mr. Sullivan for a few weeks until Laura decided that treating him like other guys was useless. You had to take charge and he would follow. It was a relationship that suited her. She had just ended a relationship with one of the male associates at her firm. It had been her usual type affair, nothing to serious, sex after the third date, and ending it when he tried treating her like she was some kind of possession. It was the standard three to six months and then on to someone new. Either they became too possessive or they dumped her for someone new. It was the story of her life, it had started in High School. She was the smartest girl in the school, valedictorian of her senior class, but guys never dated her for her brains. Frankly they dated her for her body and she knew it. Back then the boys were rarely subtle about what attracted them.

Laura's problem now was that she was still working long hours for the law firm and most men did not want a relationship that played so distant a second to her work. The alternative was to pick up some guy who would view her as a meal ticket. She did not want that kind of companion. She could have all the casual sex she wanted, but she wanted a man who would hold her and love her. She would do anything for a loving relationship. She could only dream of that guy who would love her and marry her. He had no face and she was beginning to think he never would.

The first two times she was officially out on a date with Pat both Steven and Susan were there; it helped keep the conversation going. Susan did most of the talking, but the dates went well, things never got tense. It was the third date, the time she normally let the man bed her that everything changed.

Patrick had picked the restaurant it was an Arab place on Atlantic Avenue in Brooklyn-his home ground. The food was good. They started with an appetizer of chickpeas and yogurt. The main course was chicken. She had no idea what it was called, but it was wonderful. Desert was Baklava, straight from heaven, and the thickest, darkest coffee she had ever had. Pat didn't eat all that much. He seemed to concentrate on seeing that she had a good time.

After dinner they strolled down to the Brooklyn Promenade, the raised walk above the express way. It has the view you see in the movies of the Manhattan skyline glittering in the night. As they walked hand-in-hand, he suddenly turned and kissed her. There wasn't an electric charge that passed between them. It was a warm inner glow she felt. She looked into his eyes and saw something she had never seen in a man's eyes before. She could not place his look. When he kissed her again, she felt a slight physical pain in her chest.

SIR PATRICK BIJOU

The evening didn't end in bed. They just walked, hardly talking. It was the most romantic evening of her life. The warm welcoming park, the shimmering city across the dark water, and the tall, handsome man who would occasionally pause their stroll to take her into his strong arms and kiss her.

The next morning waking alone in bed she had this sense of joy that she could not place. Half between sleep and being awake, it came to her. The look in his eyes was love, not lust. Every other male, man and boy, had lusted for her. They wanted to fuck her. Pat wanted to love her. Her joy was tinged with fear. Did he see her for the kind of women she was? She made up her mind to take things slow to hold back in case this was just another three months, and we are done thing. She was not sure she could take that. It would mean there was no reality to her dream of a home and family.

It soon became apparent that Patrick was a different kind of guy. He knew the demands she faced with her work and adjusted his life to hers. It meant that she found herself for the first time in a relationship where she called all the shots and it didn't seem to faze the guy at all. She was older almost 27 to his 21. He had almost two years left in law school, but that just meant that he was all the more available to her. The only significant friend he had was Steven, which worked out well because Susan and she were quick to bond. The four of them did a lot together which suited Laura. She had few close friends in New York because of the excessive demands of her work. It also meant she could keep some distance between the affection that Pat showered her with and the insecurity she felt.

Susan seemed to be in the same boat when it came to close friends. She knew everyone but didn't keep people around her. Susan confessed that she had trouble making friends with women because of her looks and found most men felt the need to bed her. Steven, she maintained, was different they had a relationship that was not dependent on sex. She could talk to him or more accurately at the perpetually silent man. Their conversation was all Susan rambling happily on until Steven said some remarkably insightful thing which would cause Susan to pause and reflect.

Neither boy was into sports. In fact they hated spectator sports. The best way to get them to leave a room was to turn on the TV to a sporting event. On the other hand, they played a lot of games, physical, and intellectual. They were mediocre students at best, but mock trial was sacred, once every week or so they would have a competition. They were unavailable for two days before and at least the day after. Finally Laura managed to see one of their competitions. She was really excited for two reasons, she would see her man in action and maybe get to finally meet Edward Kincade. Ironically they were matched against her alma mater, Yale. She figured the boys would get beat, but she hoped not too bad.

She was wrong. Oh, it was a slaughter, but it was Yale that got beat. Teams could be two or three student lawyers. Brooklyn had three Patrick, an Asia girl and

SIR PATRICK BIJOU

Steven. Patrick opened his presentation timed to the second, clear and so lucid. Yale opened well but was a definite second from the start. By the time Steven closed it was a rout. Laura sat in her seat amazed. It was as if she were watching two different people. The shy Patrick she knew was not in attendance. In his place was a sure and masterful advocate who stood as the center of attention and held his dominant place against all comers. She began to wonder who this Patrick was and where did he come from.

Laura did get introduced to Ed Kincade, who was as proud as a parent. His men, as he called them, did him proud again and you could feel Patrick and Steven's pride in his praise. That night Laura took Pat back to her apartment. She had half a mind to make love to him, but he got sick: chills and vomiting. She put him to bed in her bed and lay herself down beside him just holding him. It seemed to help and in the morning, he was better but tired. Over the weeks that followed she saw the pattern repeat itself. Sick after the event and tired the next day. When she related this to Susan, she said that Steven was exhausted after as well, but did not get sick, just the shakes.

"It must take a lot out of them becoming someone else like that," Susan said.

Laura could only wonder, she knew she would never make a trial lawyer, but she was sure this was not normal. One day she ran into John Stringer, III in the elevator.

He was third generation lawyer and did some trial work in his youth.

"Mr. Stringer," she said with trepidation, the young associate talking to the most senior partner.

"Yes Laura?" he said breaking into a broad grin at her surprise that he knew her name. But thinking I am not so old I do not know the name of the prettiest and sexiest associate we've had in the last twenty years.

"Well, it's my boyfriend. You see he does mock trials and is very good." But she hesitated not clear how she should go on.

"BUT?" he queried.

"Well he gets kind of sick to his stomach after."

He started chuckling and said: "Oh, to be young again, Laura he has stage fright."

"But he gets sick after?"

"Yes, butterflies in the gut before and after they get released as he cools down."

"Does it eventually go away?" she asked.

"No, you just get use to it, or you take up commercial finance," he said giving her a wink. The elevator stopped and he left, but he turned as he did and said, "Don't be a stranger, if you ever need help you know where I am."

Susan was getting married. She was rather proud that she had maneuvered Steven into a proposal. He had barely got the words out before she had the date picked.

"I think a June wedding is traditional. His exams will be over by then and I can arrange a two-week vacation plus get the advantage of the Fourth of July weekend if I work it right," she explained to Laura.

"Yes, but he'll still have a year of school left."

"Oh Laura, you don't think he's going to support me. I've money for both of us."

"But he's so young Susan."

"At twenty-two he's plenty old enough and I'm past twenty-seven. Time I was married."

Susan was not hearing any disagreement and in a way she was right. They were in love, why wait? Steven would never earn what she did as a Junior Partner in New York's Gary Partners, what some believed was the top PR firm in the nation. After school he would be lucky to land a job paying fifty thousand a year. Susan already made five times that and had family resources that were beyond substantial. She had a top flight career. Like Laura, Susan had attended the best schools and was in a great career position. There was no way that Steven could ever compete. In fact one of his best qualities is that he didn't try. He was content playing the supportive partner.

"So are you up to blowing off some steam?" Susan asked.

"How so?"

"You, me, and Steven's sister Lisa, I say we party every chance we get until I tie the knot."

Laura knew Lisa. She was a taller female version of her brother at just under six feet. She was bean pole thin. She was nineteen and had been a working runway model for four years. Laura knew what blowing off steam with Lisa meant. She was almost as physically attractive as her brother but unlike him no virgin.

"Susan, out with you two I would feel like an ugly duckling."

"Oh, sure Ms. I'm too sexy for my shirt. We'll have guys crawling all over the three of us."

That began the longest hen party in history. Every chance the three women had to get together outside work and away from their men they proceeded to party. A typical evening began at an uptown singles bar where the men would line up for the chance to hit on them. The place could be filled with single women and the three of them would be monopolizing the men. Susan, as Laura soon learned, was exceedingly picky. She liked them big, muscular and well dressed. She went for confident men who put themselves out there. It made Laura wonder what she saw in Steven.

"Oh, it's simple he has everything I want to come home to, good looks, a pleasant personality, and true love. I know he loves me and always will, and I never need to worry about our fighting over bullshit like with every other guy. What I want is fine with him. He leaves my life to me, and he's so self-contained that you never need to worry about him. Whatever I have to give him is all he ever wants. How few men there are who will make sacrifices for your career over their own. Steven is there for me."

Laura realized she could have said the same about Pat.

"Susan, with the kind of money your family has why are you so driven to succeed?"

"Oh, you naive girl. The deVoe family money was all but gone when mom married dad. She had the name and a few bucks he could start a business with. My dad is a gambler, a good one, but just a gambler. The family business isn't insurance as people think, but reinsurance, the big risks on the long odds. Dad is the casino owner not the sucker betting at the table, but sooner or later the double zero comes up three times in a row. We have had our broke periods every few years since I was a little girl. My big sister, Mary, remembers even worse than I do.

Dad goes up big, but he goes down big as well. I have to be able to fend for myself."

Laura could only think that you just never know. In theory she understood reinsurance. The practice employed by the big insurance carriers to cover extraordinarily high risks and big liability situations such as sky scrapers and major commercial ventures. The carriers spread the risk wide and charge for the average risk while trying to cherry pick the lowest risk customers. Set the rate on one in a hundred and only cover the one in a thousand risk customers. Reinsurance was more a gamble, big bets on much more limited numbers, but bigger profits on higher risks.

One night they took a limo from the upper West Side back to Susan's Chelsea Condo with three studs in tow. Laura's man was tall and well built without being musclebound. He was a stock broker and had bragged for most of the night about his financial prowess. He was older in his early thirties and black. Susan's fellow had a Scandinavian accent. He was very tall and claimed to come originally from Denmark. He now worked at the UN as an interpreter. His attitude seemed to be that all American girls were easy. The last of the three had gravitated to Lisa. He was the shortest about five feet eleven but built like a brick house and wide in the shoulders and the butt. He claimed to be a professional hockey player in town for some kind of post-season activity. He had a Mediterranean complexion with a broad Midwestern accent.

Susan's Condo had three bedrooms, although one was converted into an office, it still had a convertible couch. Lisa grabbed her hockey player and headed for the office. Susan pulled the Dane into her bedroom and Laura and the black stock broker took the second bedroom.

His arms wrapped around her waist and he pulled her toward him. Their lips met with all the heat that they had been building as they flirted that night. His hands slid down to cup her ass and pull her against his hardness. They shed his pants as Laura's dress hit the floor. She had on lacy red underwear that she had been sure to never let Pat see. As far as he knew she was a good girl. Nor was she thinking of Pat just then. She had a big stud to play with. He was nowhere near the first or even her first black man. She moaned as his hand pushed her legs apart and raced to where the lace was soaked by the fluid seeping from her lower lips. He pushed her bra up and sucked in her nipples moving from one to the other. She had big breasts for the size of her body, and he gave them his attention. Her nipples became rock hard and she was reaching overdrive way too fast.

"Please FUCK ME!" she begged slipping down her panties. She still had her stockings on and kicked off the fuck me pumps as he grabbed her legs and spread them over his shoulders. She guided him to her sex where he gave one hard trust and sank deep into her. One more thrust and he bottomed out. He had barely begun when she erupted in an intense orgasm. A moment later he came. They lay together on the bed gasping for breath. She gave him some time to recoup before she began the effort to arouse him again. She hated giving a man oral sex, although she preferred cunnilingus to intercourse. In college, she had tried swapping one for the other, but while guys like getting it, they rarely give it with any skill. It was the best way to rouse a man so she moved down to his flaccid penis and began stroking it before licking it. She took him into her mouth working him back to hardness. She was crouched on the bed, his revived penis half in her mouth when Susan Spoke.

"Care for a switch?" she said standing in the doorway, naked holding the big Dane by his long thin cock.

Laura sat up as Susan casually led the Dane to the bed and swapped him out for the black man. So the night went, swapping partners and fucking hard cocks until four in the morning when they had all ended up in Susan's bed. Susan casually chased the guys out saying she needed some sleep before her fiancé showed up. In fact they spent the time cleaning and showering so that when Steve and Pat showed up at seven-thirty, they were sitting around the kitchen table in fluffy white bath robes all clean and smelling fresh.

Susan had got clean away with it, but Laura had a bad case of guilt. She had never done anything as depraved as last night before, leaving her to wonder if she was now officially a slut, which was nothing as compared to how she thought Patrick would think of her, if he knew. Would he even want to see her again knowing the kind of woman she was?

SIR PATRICK BIJOU

She hadn't betrayed him! They were not engaged nor did they have any formal arrangement. She told herself they were simply two people who dated. They had never had sex. She saw him as too young and inexperienced. She had not fallen so far as to lead him that far astray! If they were to consummate their relationship, it would have far more meaning then a wild night of sex to someone as virtuous and sensitive as Pat. That said she knew what she had done was wrong. She needed sex, but she needed to be the kind of woman Pat deserved if she was to stay with him.

Laura got up from the table and gave Pat a hug and a kiss and led him off into the second bedroom where they lay snuggling on the bed. It was there-and-then that she decided no more casual sex and that her relationship with Pat needed to move forward, slowly so as not to scare him off, but forward until they were true lovers. She would respect his purity, but it would have to yield to the passion of their mutual love because now, in the full knowledge of her own shortcomings, she knew just how much she loved this man.

Susan's wedding to Steven was held in New Canaan, Connecticut two weeks later. Susan was the proverbial vision in white. The wedding was a big affair, but it was mostly relatives of her mother and business associates of her father. Susan had actually few women friends and she was not about to invited a string of old lovers. Laura was drafted as a bridesmaid since Pat was the best man. Susan's older sister Mary was maid of honor. Two deVoe family twin sisters and Lisa completed the bride's side.

Susan's brother Robert, Mary's husband, Jason and two deVoe cousins were the groomsmen. The wedding went as smooth as silk and Susan and Steve left for two weeks in Paris. She had been there before; he had never left New York before he met Susan.

Laura had arranged for herself and Pat to stay in the Roger Sherman Inn, a small cozy place off the Main Street. She had checked them in as husband and wife, giggling as she did so. Mr. And Mrs. Sullivan spent their first night chastely sharing a room with a big queen-sized bed.

Laura planned the night of the wedding to be different. At the reception Laura made sure Pat had something to drink but not too much. She had stayed away from all alcohol. When they arrived back at the inn after the wedding, she was ready.

She needed help with the teal bridesmaid dress. Could he get the zipper? She had slipped her bra and panties off before she left the reception. When she stepped out of the dress she was wearing just a garter belt, stockings, and heels. She didn't pause, but began helping him out of his clothes.

She pushed him down on the bed; it was not hard at that moment, a feather would have knocked him over. He was hard and he moaned as her hand found his cock. She marveled at how hot he was. She was hot as well: hotter than she could ever remember being. She could feel this was different; it wasn't just sex. She wanted him-no she needed-him to love her. As she crawled up onto him, she planted kisses on his body.

He was passive at first, then the ice melted under the fire of her passion. He embraced her in two powerful arms. She had a momentary thought of the contrast between how soft his skin felt and how hard his body was. How odd she thought.

Laura seemed to lose herself in his kisses. He began to kiss her nipples that felt as hard as steel, but yielded to his lips and tongue. She pushed his head down-she wanted it between her legs. She climbed him till her lower lips touched his upper lips. He had no idea what to do. She ground her herself against his mouth until he caught on. Then she got into a sixty-nine position and began licking his cock. The more she licked, the more aggressive he became. Finally, he pushed her over and moved between her legs. It took him a fumbling minute to find the entrance and then he impaled her. She expected quick. He fooled her again. He fucked her to two orgasms and was still going. Each time she thought he was there he seemed to fall back.

"Don't hold back. I want to feel you come in me," she said.

CHAPTER FOUR

He stroked in faster and then faster still. It built and built, she shook with another orgasm, letting out a scream she was sure they heard all over the Inn. That had certainly never happened to her before, and then he came and came. She saw a perplexed look in his eyes. He was on top now and looking down at her.

"You alright Baby?" she asked.

"Yes, but are we protected?"

She laughed and said, "On the Pill my love, Oh my sweet love."

July had become August and the summer was gone. Patrick had to return to school as did Steven, who was now living in Chelsea with Susan. Laura began pushing for Patrick to move in with her.

"It will mean more time together," she argued.

"But..." he trailed off without saying it.

"What! You don't mind screwing me but don't want people to know?" she said knowing she was not being fair. He didn't want to tell his very Catholic parents he was sleeping with her and she understood. On the other hand she loved this man and wanted him to marry her, and not someday but now. She had come around to Susan's way of a thinking-there was no point in waiting-she was ready and whether he liked it or not, he was hers.

"Laura, please let's try to work something out?" he pleaded

"OK, but I love you and want to be with you. Of all people, you should understand how difficult the hours in my job are," she said, her voice and her face begging, but beneath the pleading was an accusation that he didn't love her enough. Laura had started manipulating Patrick and it was a pattern that was to last.

She knew if she kept building the pressure, he would see his only way out was to propose. An engagement would give them the requisite respectability. He would think he could put off the wedding quite a while, but she would squelch that soon enough.

He cracked about two weeks into the new school year. He nearly ran himself ragged trying to be with her and make it back and forth between his parent's home and school. She made it as hard as possible till he gave in.

The engagement ring was small only half a carat. It took every penny he could scrape together. Most of the funds came from card games in the student cafeteria. He and Steven left no sucker unfleeced. They would have a hard time finding a game the rest of their law school careers. One of the suckers was Ed Kincade. His game was bridge but he was no match for Steven even when he demanded that Pat sit one rubber as his partner. Kincade hated to lose as much as Steven did.

Small as the ring was Laura treasured it. She took Pat home to meet her family, her mother, father and three younger sisters. Her family loved Pat. She was the oldest by seven years. Then the next three had come one after the other. Her father longed for a son. She knew her dad was looking for that in Pat, but feared Pat was to quirky and not very into guy kind of things.

Once again Pat surprised her. When her Dad talked sports Pat stayed right with him. Oh, he didn't know the player's names or the statistics, but he knew the intimate mechanics of each sport, what you needed to win and what would cause you to lose. It came out that there was virtually no game that he and Steven had played that Steven had not figured a way to cheat at.

The family was in no position to fund a big wedding, but that is not what Laura wanted. She kept it small and simple. The honeymoon was in Las Vegas, it was cheap. Four days over Veterans' Day. Patrick won five thousand at black jack and the management began looking at him funny. Susan and Steven flew in for the last two days, and the four of them had a good time. By Tuesday she was back, hard at work.

Two years later she announced to Pat that they were moving to Albany. He had graduated, taken the bar and passed the first time, but had no job. The Senior Associate position for municipal bonds had opened in the Albany Office and Laura smelled a partnership opportunity. Such openings had become very few following the recession. So they moved.

When they got to Albany Laura announced that she wanted to put down roots. The housing market had just crashed. She saw the opportunity to buy a house. He found work with the Van Patten County DA part-time covering Village Night Court. So Redmond, a rather nice suburb of Albany in Van Patten County, was the spot she chose and she found a nice 2200 square foot ranch in a mid-size development. Patrick went along.

He didn't like his job, but apparently, they liked him. He was moved into a full-time position within a year, but the job paid crap. However, everything was fine until Frank Patterson showed up.

Patterson was a tall well-built exceedingly handsome man in his mid-forties. He was a senior partner, a Harvard Law graduate. He was the kind of masterful male that turned women on. He had started in the firm's Washington office, but been bounced around to every office until he reached Albany. From the very first, he was friendly with Laura. He complemented her clothes, her work, and most of all her looks. He was flirting. It was flattering, but she was married. She didn't flirt back, not at first. He was not deterred.

Laura was in a bind. Brentwood Stringer as a firm had taken a hit in the national economic collapse which meant that fewer partnerships were given out. Laura was overdue. She had moved to the Albany office to better her chances in the smaller pond and to move into municipal finance where the profits were high at the time.

She couldn't just reject Patterson and she certainly could not make a scene or ask for help from above, that would kill her chances. She was on the knife's edge of a very big dilemma.

In the end, she chose to play along. It wasn't just for her; it was for Pat and the family that she told herself they both wanted. Though Pat had never said anything about kids other than that first time they had sex worrying that they were not protected.

If she brought up starting a family Pat would talk about it. She talked about having a large family. Pat never brought it up on his own. Well he was a guy and younger than her and his fertility was not running out. She needed the partnership and she needed it now.

Patterson found her weakness, it wasn't hard to spot. She was desperate for her name on the partners' side of the letterhead. He dangled it and eventually the fish bit on the bait. It still took him until the firm's Christmas Party to set the hook. When he met Pat that evening he wondered what all the fuss was about, that wimp would do nothing. He would probably thank Frank for fucking his wife. Patterson had to laugh.

The first-night Frank had Laura to his house he took her right to his bedroom and forced her to her knees. As he stood over her she sucked his cock till he came in her mouth. He was showing her who was in charge. On the next date he took her ass something she hadn't done before; then he knew her husband was a wimp. Frank had nothing but contempt for men like Pat Sullivan. They were second rate. Their women were up for grabs, and they could do nothing about it. He made it a practice to bed as many of the women he worked with as he could. He preferred the married ones because he got a kick out of making their husbands cuckolds. This had caused problems and he had been moved from office to office. They hadn't fired him because he had a senior partner's slot that he had gained through internal politics. Until now none of the complaints about his activities had been formal. He was expecting no trouble when he was done with Laura.

Laura had not been happy with the relationship from the first. The sex was not great-only different. Frank tried to be too dominating in the bedroom. She enjoyed submitting to his physical dominance on a base level, but she also enjoyed being on top and playful carefree sex as well. Ultimately he was too old and heavy handed.

OFFENCE AND JUSTICE

By February their affair was almost over, Frank was sure she would break it off after the partnership meeting if she got the nod. He tried to quietly see if he could block it, but that Jew Solomon was adamant that she had earned it as were the senior partners in the City, surprisingly headed by Mr. Stringer himself. So Frank was resigned to seeing how it would end with Laura. She gave him one last taste on Presidents' Day and told him that she thought her husband might be suspicious and she would need to break it off. He did not believe that story until the husband confronted him and all hell broke loose.

The Cops stopped Frank within a mile of the Bar he had been drinking in. Sullivan had approached him at the close of his weekly networking meeting. Frank had few clients that he could call his own. He had been trying to build a client base in case the firm tried to ease him out. He knew Solomon in particular was watching him. He could afford no public scandal. When Pat Sullivan sat down at the table he knew that things might get complicated. He was relieved that the cuckold husband was trying to avoid exposure, that made good sense. Sullivan would not want it public that he could not hold on to his wife. So he played along, drinking and talking about the need to keep things quiet. He did not notice the waitress being overly attentive and filling and refilling the glasses.

Frank should have called a cab, but he headed out driving super careful along a route he knew by heart. But the Cops were waiting-Van Patten County Sherriff's Deputies. They were all business. They took him to a

Podunk town court where they ushered him right in. It still didn't register that he had been arrested until they asked if he wished to contact a lawyer and suddenly Steven Fitzgerald a prominent defense attorney was beside him. Steven led him into a room and explained the facts of the situation. In short, he was truly screwed, but he could get out of it for a mere two hundred thousand dollars. At first, he didn't believe it.

Patrick Sullivan the wimpy husband had set him up and was extorting him for money. Frank pretty much spent what he earned. He had a big expensive colonial house and a Mercedes-Benzes SLS GT with the extras almost a quarter million in car. A boat on the river and a summer camp in the Adirondacks. To raise the two hundred thousand he would need to draw cash from his retirement which would have a tax consequence. That dam Sullivan was going to make him down-size his lifestyle. Frank did not enjoy being pushed around by some kid from Brooklyn-a lousy little Assistant County DA. In the scheme of things, he saw himself as being entitled and Sullivan as the kind of man who was required to yield to him. Somehow the wimpy husband had got the best of him, but Frank would get even.

June was Laura's secretary/administrative assistant. She knocked on her boss's office door. June knew Patrick, and has always said how lucky Laura was to have him. Laura wonders how lucky June thinks she is now.

"Mr. Solomon wants to see you," June said with a look of concern on her round face. "Are you alright Laura? Should I tell him you need a minute?" she asked.

"No, I'm alright."

Laura walked through the office not looking left or right and headed for the elevators to take her to the floor above. Saul Solomon had a large office on the building's fifth floor. It was alternatively used as a meeting room for important clients and the Government Affairs Group, which is the name given to the firm's division that was responsible for lobbying the State and Federal Governments.

Margaret, Saul's executive assistant, told Laura to go right in, he was expecting her. As she entered, she was at first blinded by the sunlight coming through the floor-to-ceiling windows. They faced west and the sun was now positioned to come at you from directly behind Saul's big desk. He wasn't at the desk, he was seated off to one side of the office where two comfortable leather chairs and a small sofa made a conversational group. On a small coffee table he had a teapot and two china cups set out.

"Come sit with me Laura and tell me how you take your tea."

He waved her to the sofa next to his chair and began fussing with the tea. She was very nervous. She knew enough about Saul to realize he was at his most dangerous when he seemed to be most gracious.

"Mr. Solomon, I want to say I am sorry for all the..."

He cut her off with a wave of his hand before she could finish.

"The apology is due from me," he said

"And it is 'Saul' to my partners Laura," he put down his cup and leaned back in his chair folding his hands over his stomach.

"You see I knew of Frank Patterson's predilections. I took precautions to protect the junior staff, but I failed to warn you or to accord you the same protection. I assumed that you were beyond his reach and well..." he paused, "able to handle him."

"I should have realized the precarious nature of your home situation. I don't mean to seem racist here but Irishmen can be very emotional in some situations. I assume that Mr. Sullivan over-reacted to your little dalliance and took some excessive measures," he said with a bit of a chuckle.

She had to give a small laugh in spite of her feelings. Saul had a way of scaling down the biggest problems to the trivial.

"Yes, his reaction was something beyond excessive, but I doubt he sees it that way."

"As I said Irishmen can let their emotions get away from them. I take it he did much more then hurt Frank's pride?" he said raising an eyebrow.

"Let's just say Frank was hurt very bad."

"Good. Maybe this will be a lesson learned. He is here as a kind of last resort. We can't keep moving him around every time one of his indiscretions gets out of hand. After all there is the liability issue to consider."

"But now," he said, "We come to you. Laura, you are my partner, I know that, in this age of corporate firms, the PCs and the LLCs, we do not give much thought to what it means to be a partner. I don't follow the norm. Being my partner means your business is also my business and my business is yours. I do not see that relationship ending at the office door. As in this case the fall-out into this office is very clear. So first, I need to move you. Starting tomorrow, you are assigned to Governmental Affairs and Jim Smallwood will take your place in Municipal Finance."

"But I know nothing about lobbying and won't Jim see Municipals as a step down?"

Now Saul laughed.

"First, having a truly beautiful woman with you when you lobby is no disadvantage, and second you don't know much about Jim if you think he will not see this as his chance to push Frank Patterson to the curb and take his senior partnership."

She had to give Saul his due. He could fall in a vat of shit and come out spotless.

"Thank you. I will endeavor to do my best," she said putting her tea down and beginning to rise.

"Sit down," he said taking up her cup and pouring some more tea.

"We still have to sort out your husband. If only to show that no one gets the best of us."

"Oh please Mr. Solomon, don't do anything to Patrick, I caused him enough pain. I just wish I could take it all back."

Saul smiled, "I was hoping all was not lost. I like your husband. So lets see what we can do to return him to you. I believe that would be best all around."

"But he's divorcing me. He made me sign a settlement agreement."

"Young woman this is the most talented and influential firm in New York. One lone Irishman isn't going to get the best of us." Saul did not let on that he and Jack Stringer had determined to block the divorce at all costs.

Jack did not believe that you divorced at the first bit of trouble in a marriage, and he told Saul flat out:

"I've seen the two of them together. The boy is way immature and he has a bad temper. He holds it in but it can be seen seething there beneath the surface. Still, it is obvious he loves her and she loves him. If we can make the boy grow up this can work out."

"Alright Jack I will hold this divorce up, and hope this kid grows up."

Saul looked at Laura and said:

"You have friends in this firm and we feel your husband just needs some time to reconsider."

With that he picked up the phone and called the head of the matrimonial and family law group, Angela Zink. They talked a few minutes, and decided Laura needed to ask for counseling before the divorce could become final. There was no doubt they could get the Judge to order it. Next he punched in a long distance call.

"Hello Bella," he said. She could only hear one side of the conversation, but they spoke about the situation, Laura found herself in. There was some discussion of methods of handling her problem. Then he made arrangements for Laura to meet with Bella Moskowitz, the best marriage counselor anywhere he assured her. Unfortunately, she was in New York City and Laura would have to travel there.

When Laura left Saul's office she felt like a new person. She had hope again and she saw her situation in a new perspective. With the help, Saul was giving her maybe she had a chance of getting Patrick back.

Governor Kincade was trapped in his Albany office; it was the second week of April and spring had arrived in New York City. However, the weatherman was predicating snow in Albany. By some as yet unknown set of circumstances, the legislature was preparing to pass the Governor's budget as he submitted it in January, virtually without change. This effort was surprisingly being led by his republican opponent State Senator Tilden. Ed Kincade was suspicious. It seemed that as the poet Browning said: 'morning's at seven—God's in his heaven-all was right with the world.' In fact, it was ten in the evening, and Don Pleasant wanted to see him.

"Send him in," the Governor said to his administrative assistant Betty.

Don walked right through the office and walked into the Governor's bathroom where he turned on the faucets full blast. The Governor followed him in closing the door.

"Patrick Xavier Sullivan, only child, St Gregory's School, Xavier High School, Fordham University, Brooklyn Law, and now ADA in Van Patten County. Married to Laura Parker Yale, Law grad, partner Brentwood & Stringer," Don paused then he smiled.

"One devious, gutsy, and smart son of a bitch," Don said, his grin said more; said he liked the bastard.

It took Don about forty minutes to lay out all he had found out about the infidelity and the extortion of Frank Paterson. The bribes were just speculation, but the money had certainly been received by Kondos and was expected by LeCour.

Governor Kincade was speechless. He would never have expected that of Patrick Sullivan.

"Can we prove any of it?" the Governor asked.

"Not a chance! That Fitzgerald is not called foxy for nothing. You have a better chance of finding Jimmy Hoffa."

"Thanks, Don."

"Any Time Gov, and If I may say so, I like the Kid's style. Sullivan is all right in my book, but not that Fitzgerald son-of-a- bitch."

Kincade knew Don's advice was good, and he needed to watch Foxy Fitzgerald who had a set of morals that were totally different from the rest of humanity. To Steven the world was full of gray shades. There was no clear right and wrong. Foxy was dangerous because he saw both sides and believed in both sides. Sullivan was different. He was just as smart but he believed in a clear right and wrong. Pat was the kind of man you could rely on to do the right thing, but now he had clearly crossed the line into wrong territory. The questions were if and when he would cross back and if he did not, could he be of use?

"Betty, get me Arnie on the phone," the Governor asked.

It was near midnight when Betty reached Arnold Flecher, the Governor's Appointments secretary.

"Governor, Denise says you are not allowed to call me after 9 p.m."

Denise was Arnie's wife and she had begun to set down rules.

"Arnie tell Denise it is an emergency. I need Patrick X. Sullivan appointed interim DA of Van Patten County first thing tomorrow morning."

"Who the fuck is this guy?"

"He is my trump and he can take an ace. I don't expect you to understand that Arnie. I'm just putting him into position to use him if I need him."

CHAPTER FIVE

P atrick

I am Patrick Sullivan, husband of Laura Parker. I guess the fact that she doesn't use my name says something about our relationship. Trouble was, until recently, I have been rather blind and deaf when it came to 'she who is soon to be my ex-wife.' Consider me one of the poor saps who get blinded by a real beauty only to wake up realizing he has made a big mistake.

Currently, I am sitting in a courtroom, usually my favorite kind of place, but not today, since I am the client, not the attorney. My attorney, Geoffrey Davis (call me Jeff), is explaining my case to Judge Roxanne Clearmont known affectionately throughout the Van Patten Courthouse as Rocky. Not after the fictional boxer, but the cartoon squirrel. I cannot say precisely why she has this nick name. Maybe it is that high grating voice she has.

Rocky is not listening to good old Jeff, whose principle qualities are that he is competent and reasonably priced. My wife's lawyer is another creature altogether. Angela Zink is a tall, cool blond in her mid-forties who could and is definitely trying to pass for thirty. She is not wearing the typical female lawyer uniform of dark pinstripes and black hose. Angela is dressed in a champagne-colored dress that falls to just below the knees and has a high lace collar. She is elegant and feminine and just by the by RUTHLESS.

I have been in enough courtrooms to know when I have been ambushed. So take my word, this is an ambush. It should have been simple enough. The separation agreement was signed. It was an unfair settlement, but at the time, it was signed I was in a very angry mood, and I did hold all the cards. I was threatening to put her boyfriend into the slammer. Yes I am a cuckold. Nonetheless, I expected to have to deal with my wife's people, and my temper had cooled, so Jeff was empowered to negotiate.

Laura had another plan. I knew that when she showed up in a new dress. It was not that it was new. It was what can best be described as a Suzie Homemaker dress. An 'Oh I bake cookies for the holidays as presents' kind of look. Her hair was back in a ponytail and she was sniffling into a tissue. Angela was kind enough to provide a box of tissues. Laura does not bake. Before we started living together, I am not sure she knew what a kitchen was. Her family joked about her lack of domestic abilities. She has three sister, and they all make fun of her household skills. She is one high-powered bond attorney and not the least bit ashamed that she is no housewife.

I grabbed Jeff, "Put her on the stand, I guarantee she won't last five minutes."

Jeff could only look at me with frustration. He was getting his clock cleaned as it was.

"You have something to add here Mr. Sullivan?" Rocky asked.

"Your honor I was just asking my attorney to show the court that despite the way my wife appears today she is a very competent attorney not an abandoned housewife."

"The court is well aware of the parties' occupations. So let me remind you Mr. Sullivan this is not a criminal trial. There is not guilt or innocence here, there is only a troubled marriage," Rocky paused and then lowered the boom on me.

"I am persuaded that the parties may have separated in haste. The current law allows me to order counseling inappropriate cases. Since counseling is something that Mrs. Sullivan has already begun with, I might add, a nationally recognized counselor, and since she has agreed to cover the entire expense, I will order counseling here," she said and then mumbled something.

Jeff jumped up and was fool enough to ask what the judge had said that he had not heard.

"I said counseling once a week until such time as the court is satisfied."

Jeff was going to protest that he had never heard of such a thing, but I grabbed his elbow and stopped him.

"We've been hosed. The fix was in," I said, "No use crying." Then I nodded at Laura and her attorney and gave my best 'it isn't over yet smile.'

It took me two weeks to get a written order and then only after I threaten not complying unless I received it in writing. My friend Steven Fitzgerald looked over the order from Judge Rocky Clearmont with me.

"Well, you have to admire Saul Solomon. He is one hell of a smart lawyer," Steve said shaking his head.

"You will forgive me if I find him a little less than admirable at this moment."

"Hey-Hey! Are you forgetting we're the bad guys here-he has truth, justice and the American way of life on his side not to mention most of the judges in this state."

"I don't see why he had to get involved." We were under no illusions that Laura had finessed the order for marriage counseling on her own. The logical opponent was the Zink bitch, but it had taken only a little asking around in the Courthouse grapevine to find out that Judge Clearmont had lunch with the Chief Administrative Judge the day before the hearing. Pull on that level had to come from a very powerful person indeed.

"You humiliated your wife and her lover both of whom are partners in his firm. People know you fucked them.

The fact that no one can prove anything as long as Laura and Frank keep their mouths shut doesn't make what you did any less humiliating," Steve said.

"But this order is ridiculous it could never be sustained," I said.

"Patrick please tell me all this time you've spent in the DA's office hasn't rotted your brain?"

"No. I realize he does not need to win. He is playing for time, but how long can this hold things up," I said pointing to the order.

"Depends on what you do. The order says marriage counseling paid for by the other side with a report back in a month. It also selects the counselor who is well known and highly qualified. But it sets no end date and requires extensive travel. It further selected a counselor acceptable to your wife, but not you-all excellent appeal issues. Interesting issues designed to give a Court justification for spend time writing.

"Ok so how do I fight the big law firm with all the influence?"

"We play along. In six months I move the case back onto the calendar before good old Rocky."

"What makes her act then?"

"Certiorari -either she grants the divorce or we take her up for not deciding. Even if Saul tries to hold us up in the appellate court, we can force a decision and there is only one possible decision here—right!" Steven reasoned this out for me.

"As usual you're correct. I see it, but I hate to get pushed around like this."

"So how's this pride thing working out for you?" I could only grumble in response.

"Look this is the price you pay for revenge. I hope it's worth it," he said.

On the Second Tuesday in April, I found myself in an office building off Fifth Avenue in New York City. I had traveled down by train that morning- round trip ticket cost was $102. Not that much but over four hundred dollars monthly, just enough to break the budget of a poor ADA. They figured I would reach for the money I extorted from Patterson, and they would have me. I had to smile at how they underestimated me.

The address of the building was a respectable walk from Penn Station, but not impossible. The meeting was held on the seventh floor of an eleven story building. The office I eventually walked into was about as non-threatening as you could get. Magazines on the end tables mixed with coloring books and crayons. There was not a receptionist or secretary, a sign said to ring a bell which is what I did. A sixtyish woman in a hunter green dress that went to her ankles let me in. The inner room had four oversized stuffed chairs and a small coffee table. A small desk was pushed against the far wall. It was not a large room and it was lit and decorated to give a warm intimate feel.

Laura was already there. It was clear that the two had been speaking and I was in no doubt what the subject of the conversation was.

"Hello, Patrick, my name is Bella. I prefer if we use only first names here. So it will be Bella, Laura and Patrick. Is that OK?" Bella said turning a pair of penetrating dark brown almost black eyes on me.

"I guess it has to be," I said

"I know you do not want to be here, but since you have to be, please give this a try. I only want to help. It would be a shame to throw away a chance at help because of pride," she said.

I just nodded.

"All right then the rules. You are expected to attend one session a week together and before that you each have a fifty minute counseling session with me to talk about whatever you want, but hopefully about why we are here." She paused then went on.

"You cannot miss a session without violating the Court Order; however if something important comes up we can reschedule. In this case because of the open order I am to report monthly to the Court. I will inform the Court when I feel you are both ready to terminate the counseling. Is that acceptable?" she said looking at me, not Laura.

I nodded my consent.

"Good, because you don't know me Patrick, let me say that I am an MD and a Ph.D. with thirty plus years in marriage counseling. I have written several books on the subject and currently teach at NYU."

"Now logistics, I am told you can be free Tuesdays Patrick, and Laura says she will make herself available that day."

"Patrick has night Court Tuesdays," Laura said like a wife casually explaining her husband's schedule as if nothing in the world was wrong.

"Tuesdays will be fine, but I need to catch the 1:20 train," I said.

"But we can drive down together," Laura said

"No!"

"No problem; there are early morning trains. I will see Laura at 9:00 a.m. then Patrick at 10:00 and finally the two of you at 11:30, that should leave Patrick plenty of time to catch his train. He can actually walk to Penn

Station from here. But Patrick you two will have homework to do together and you may on occasion find it convenient to use the travel time to accomplish that. Not a requirement, just a thought," Bella said ending that part of the meeting

"All right first I don't make judgments or assess blame. I am not here to determine whether what has happened is good or bad. Second I do not separate you into the betrayed and the betrayer. The victim and victimizer you are two people in a marriage. One of you did something that has hurt the other. You both need to deal with it and accept your share of the responsibility for what happened. Not an equal share but some portion," she said

"So she cheats and I am to blame," I said.

"Is that what I said, Patrick?" Bella asked as if she were speaking to a small child.

"What I said is that each of you has a responsibility, not equally. So you Patrick are not entirely to blame, but must share some responsibility for what happened," Bella said regaining her composure and giving me a look that said cool it buster.

"Finally, I am not here to keep you together. We will assess what is best here for the two of you. Hopefully, we can make a consensual decision as to what is best for both of you."

After this she had Laura tell her about our marriage without our discussing the infidelity. While Laura talked Bella's eyes never left me. I got the distinct impression she was trying to look into my soul.

When the session was over she walked us out, as she did she leaned into me and whispered, "Pat I know you don't want to come here, but I hope you are man enough to take advantage of this."

That said we parted. I knew what Bella wanted, she intended to destroy my pride so that I would take back Laura and become my wife's doormat. It was not going to happen.

On the train back north I switched on my phone to the internet and checked the news for something to do. The Times Union had a headline up on its web site.

UNKNOWN APPOINTED INTERIM 'DA' IN VAN PATTEN

The accompanying article gave pretty much the bare facts. When I had been admitted to the bar, where I went to law school and how long I worked in the DA's office. Not much more, they didn't have more. That I assumed would come later, speculation would abound. Let them wonder. But best of all Laura would be furious. She would know how I did it, and more I would no longer be some helpless jerk she could just push around. I was the

DA. I had a career, maybe only eight months' worth, but still for once I was somebody.

The following Tuesday morning at 10:00 o'clock, I had my first one on one with Bella Moskawitz. I arrived just as Laura left, I had waited until I saw her leave so I was a few minutes late.

Bella pointedly informed me that she expected me to be on time.

"How are you sleeping Patrick?" she asked.

"Fine, why shouldn't I be?" I asked.

"Well, you clearly engaged in actions that are morally wrong, if not criminal- although I am not an expert on that as you are," she said.

"Well I do not see any proof that I have committed some crime."

"Is that your standard now? Your wife tells me you have very high moral standards. Is she wrong?"

"When did this become about my guilt. I am not the guilty party here."

"Is that what you really believe?"

"Where are we going with this?" I asked.

"Well, I believe that you need to forgive yourself and I don't believe that you can until you forgive your wife. You see I have seen men like you before. You have betrayed yourself to avoid the pain that you felt over your wife's failing. Laura could not see how hurt you would be; it never occurred to her. I know that is hard for you to accept because your prospective is entirely different. Your wife's lack of intent does not mitigate the pain you felt. Your response was an attempt to avoid that pain, but it cannot succeed. You're only going to continue to hurt until you deal with the problem."

"I see so forgive and forget and all will be well."

"I did not say that. You need to forgive as a start and then do penance to restore your own self-respect. You can't live with yourself now and you have cut yourself off from the person who loves you the most in this world. Patrick, you are lost, let Laura help you back to where you were."

"Sorry, not buying this. She betrayed me. She gave herself to that worthless jerk. As far as I'm concerned she can stay with him."

"Fine, I am patient. You're going to come around, sooner would be better than later, but we can wait."

She was right in a sense, and I was missing Laura. The last week had been dreadful. Being what amounted to a lame duck DA was anything but easy, especially when the upper staff had reason to hate your guts for upsetting the cozy little situation they thought they had. The senior staff in the Van Patten DA's office thought they could grab the brass ring and leave the work to others. I had upset that plan. Now it was work for me or get out. They were leaving as fast as they could find any place to land. On the other hand a few looked on me as some kind of hero. Odd, that only made me feel worse like I had not earned it, somehow I stole it, which if I was honest was the truth.

"So tell me Patrick what do you tell people who ask how you became DA?" Bella asked. The woman was astute, she could hone right in on your weakness.

"Don't you read the Schenectady Gazette? I am a former student of the Governor. He is my mentor and plucked me from obscurity because he perceives my innate ability," I said, but I couldn't suppress a smirk and she had to smile with me.

"Does anyone believe that?" she asked.

"Everyone believes it to the point that it is now the truth. As we lawyers say, never confuse the facts with the truth. Facts only confuse a jury, get in the way of what they want to believe," I replied.

"I hadn't realized you were so cynical," she said.

"Live and learn."

"Just as I suspected, your wife is no more than a convenient target, the issues go much deeper don't they?"

"Your good, but this is going nowhere. She cheated end of story."

"No, I think not. You let her cheat to give yourself an excuse, a justification for your actions. Poor Laura was trapped by circumstances. She sees herself as much more responsible than you. More the dominate partner, but that is an illusion the power has always been on your side all you had to do was flex your muscle."

"You sure of that?"

"Yes, but I wonder when will you take pity on this poor girl and stop punishing her for being weaker than you are?"

"So much for my being the injured party and the responsibility being shared," I said.

"Did you think I was so blind I could not see the truth or did you intend to blind me with your lawyer tricks?"

"So she gets to bed other men and I am to just stand and watch."

"She wanted what most if not all women wanted a child. She put it off to have a career, but it was eating at her. She was easy prey for a man like Patterson. She had a husband but he refused to protect her. Perhaps he doesn't really love her?"

"I loved her and I knew I couldn't stop her. She didn't believe in me."

"So you showed her."

"Yes."

"So forgive her, it is the decent thing to do, she is in so much pain."

'The quality of mercy is not strain'd. It droppeth as the gentle rain from heaven Upon the place benieth: it is twiced blest; It blesseth him that gives and him that takes: This mightiest in the mightiest...'

"Should have known you would quote a woman lawyer, but what happens to me, how do I call myself a man if I accept this?"

She turned those dark eyes on me and said: "I believe in you Patrick you are truly brave you will not fail me. You have too much courage to be afraid of what people will think."

It was four a.m. on a Sunday morning; and, if you didn't count today, I had been DA for all of twelve days. The house on Indian Hill Road was a modest two bedroom ranch, the kind with a garage at one end that you eventually made into a bedroom or to which you added a wing to make an ell shape. It probably sold for over a hundred grand at the top of the market a few years back, but was now abandoned in the bust that followed. Until now the only crime that had ever touched, it was the mortgage fraud game played by America's largest banks and their accomplices in the Federal Reserve and the US Treasury.

Sergeant Brandt of the Sheriff's patrol met me on the front porch. He was somber in manner.

"It's in here," he said in almost a whisper leading me through the front door which led directly into the living room.

In the room's center was a headless corpse. It was a gruesome scene, and I could not shake a sense of unreality. The shag carpet was soaking up the pools of blood beneath the corpse. The carpet did not look all that old and I wondered if the former owners had agonized over the color and depth the way Laura and I had in our little house. It was now that I missed her most. She would not be there when I returned home to share this burden and add her strength and intellect to my own. There were three additional Sheriff's deputies huddled out of the way in a corner and my chief investigator squatting by the body on a dry area of carpet.

Philip Sloane was a short fat man in his sixties, who was as of eleven days ago the chief investigator of the Van Patten County DA, in other words he worked for me. He was my first appointment. He had no law enforcement back ground at all. He was a PI not a cop until about ten years ago when he took a part time position with my predecessor. We had worked together on a number of cases and I knew he was the best I had. He had no political connections but then I did not have to worry about the politics.

"Took off his head and his hands, makes identification difficult but not impossible. From the amount of blood, he was alive when they cut off his head," Phil said.

I could tell they were all watching me. There was Brandt, Sloane and the three other sheriff's deputies. I just nodded my head. I wasn't getting sick if that is what they expected.

"I had Brandt give the State Police a call and give them a set of bad directions so we would have time to look things over first. We took pictures of everything," Phil said then he reached down and picked up one of the handless arms.

"He's got needle tracks on both arms and his tats say he's a Hell's Angel. We should have no trouble identifying him."

The corpse was wearing a white tee-shirt or what use to be white and a pair of black leather pants.

"No jacket?" I asked.

"No. Either they wanted a trophy or are using it to send a message. I'd guess the latter," Phil said.

"You think drugs?"

"I suspect so, and probably a fight over the shipments up to Vermont and New Hampshire."

The drug route to Vermont went through the Capital District of New York. Van Patten wasn't usually involved, but this was clearly where someone decided to make a statement and I had, therefore, caught the black queen. The reality is that the headless corpse would make a big splash with the press, but was unlikely to get much attention from the State Police. The State Crime lab was the best, but the State Troopers were like the hats they wore, more cowboys in uniform then police. Unfortunately, we would need tremendous luck to solve this crime with the resources we had. It would be solved eventually when someone needed to trade information to get out from under another charge. That would probably take years. In the meantime, since this happened on my watch, I would be held responsible and what little chance I had in the next election would be gone.

I looked at those around me and knew that they were thinking the same thing. I had lost a lot of staff since taking over. Those that were not already gone were planning on leaving. This horrendous homicide was just another weight for me to carry.

Without Laura I was alone. Steven, my only real friend, was off doing a high profile murder case down in Westchester County. Looking around, I knew it was now that I needed to prove I could lead.

"My Dad used to say that God never sends us a problem unless he feels we're ready for it. So let's do everything we can and leave the rest to God," I said. It must have been the right thing because I saw determined smiles all around. As I left the State Police showed up. Let them just collect the evidence and not cock it up I prayed.

Katrina Gomez was acting as my secretary. Two weeks before she had been the low person in the office hierarchy, but that was before the mass exodus. I could not blame the staff-most were following what they deemed their political best interests. Katrina buzzed me that Phil Sloane was here. Phil came in carrying a stack of folders.

"Well we know our victim and have a good idea who killed him," he said setting down the folders on the oversized desk I now had as acting DA.

"Good afternoon Phil, nice to see you too," I said, he just waived a hand.

"We ain't got time for small talk. We got vultures to catch."

He then explained that the dead man was Ricky St. Simons an ex Hell's Angel. Ricky ran a string of women mostly ex-prostitutes who cleaned up well enough to pass for housewives. A deal with a local used car lot gave them access to a supply of minivans. Once or twice a week they made a run to Vermont and unloaded a shipment of Heroin.

"That's what we found in those tracks, he had: heroin," Phil said.

"So the victim is a heroin dealer?"

"No he's just the transport. The dealers are these guys."

From the stack of folders he took files on a half dozen individuals that made up the northern contingent of a black biker gang, the Vultures. They operated from New York City to Albany and were using Ricky to go the final distance into Vermont."

"It seems there was a falling out all around," Phil said

"So we have our victim and our suspects, but no case."

"Not yet, but we do have this," he said pushing the last folder across the desk to me.

The murder weapon was a machete, and the victim had lost his head while still alive. It was a weapon that had been used before, twice in NYC, but in neither case had the head been severed; however, it left what the experts considered very distinctive tool marks."

"They can identify the weapon?" I asked.

"That is what the State boys say. If we can find it!" Phil had a big grin as he said this. I could see he envisioned the trouble our finding something, that if they were stupid enough to keep it, would be well hidden. Still, it was an opportunity.

One week later, I was sitting in a bare, windowless room, little bigger than a closet. Across the small table was Kathy Lumous her big brown eyes were fixed on me and not in a nice way. I had snatched her and her youngest son, a boy of two, from the corridor outside the Department of Social Services office. We were just down the hall from the DSS office where she had just registered for her benefits and met with the employment counselor. The Sheriff's Office was responsible for the security to the DSS. Brandt worked it out to get our guys into position, so we could make the grab unobserved. Kathy's older son was almost five and in the local charter preschool. She had lily white skin and blond hair which made those dark eyes of hers all the more intense.

"Who the hell are you?" she asked the hostility showing in her voice.

She was pretty, but not beautiful. Her main attributes were those eyes and her skinny body. Percy Jackson aka P Jack but known to his intimates as PJ liked his pussy thin and white. Kathy was his northern squeeze, he had another in NYC same complexion but three kids. Kathy's two were nice brown babies. Officially they had no designated fathers, but Percy was not known to let his women loose until he was done with them. So there was strong suspicion that these boys and the three down south were Percy's.

"Miss Lumous, I am Patrick Sullivan, DA of Van Patten County."

She sniffed at this. She was putting up a tough front, but I was counting on her being smart.

"So Mr. DA what do you want?"

"Some information, just the answers to two questions."

"Do I look stupid to you?"

"No, in fact I'm hoping you will be very smart."

"Really!"

"You see I'm hoping to avoid prosecuting such a lovely young woman for welfare fraud and taking away a mother from her children."

She only smiled at this.

"You got nothing and I know it. They just brought me in because I run my five years and now my benefits are getting reduced. The Lady says I should get a job, that they will help me with my daycare and carfare. But I'm thinking that taking care of two kids is a full-time job."

She was smug, but I had her, she just didn't know it yet.

"Not so full-time. You have been going to school full-time for your nursing degree. Odd you have not reported that since Social Services would help with the daycare and the carfare for your education. Of course, you don't need carfare since you have a two year old Chevy and it might be hard to explain where the tuition and book money came from. I hear St. Rose College is pretty expensive."

"My Mom helps me."

"Except she died a year ago, but then anyone looking at her Pioneer Savings Bank account wouldn't know that," I said passing her the bank records.

"Nobody prosecutes for this kind of thing. I'm just improving myself, trying to get off welfare. The system is just stupid- it doesn't give you a chance to get out."

She was right. Van Patten's chief trial counsel until his untimely death was Tom Maitland. His ex-wife Beth worked in County DSS and was always complaining that the DA didn't prosecute welfare fraud. Trouble is outside the big cities there is almost no major fraud in the system. The locals call this area smallbany since everyone knows everyone else. Fraud, when it occurs, is small time. Someone, a little slow to report a job or a new living arrangement. The DA's office had an arbitrary limit. No prosecutions under three thousand dollars. That eliminated all but the rare case and we proceeded to work on what we perceived to be the important crimes.

"Well that was the case, but I'm making changes. I have you for failing to report assets, that is, a late model car and cash going in and out of this bank account. Are you willing to gamble that you can beat the charges?"

She looked at me hard.

"We being recorded?"

"No, do I look stupid? I just forcibly grabbed a woman and her child, how do you think that makes me look."

"Ok so what are we doing?"

"Two questions. The first is two weeks ago Saturday night who was P Jack hanging with? I figure you are his alibi and, therefore, know who he was actually with."

"No. I don't roll on PJ."

"Didn't ask you to. Just need to know who he was with. Between you and me, this goes no further since no one knows you are here with me."

"Ok." she said and I passed her a yellow legal pad and a pencil."

She wrote down the names and pushed the pad back to me.

"Last question," I said looking over the names.

"Who has the machete?"

She hesitated a long moment then circled a name and slapped the pencil down on the table.

Standing she said, "We done now?"

"Yes," I replied. I got up, went to the door and knocked, and Brandt opened it and when the coast was clear let her out. He gave me a look and I could only smile. We had the first piece.

"This one," I said pointing at the list of names to the one in the circle. "We follow him everywhere he goes."

Bella was a persistent woman. She kept on me to the point I wanted to strangle her, but I thought I had myself under control enough to handle what she threw at me. Naïve is the word for what I was. The joint session had started normally with Laura talking as usual. The private one-on-one with Bella and me at 10:00 a.m. went well. She threw a lot at me, but I managed to duck and block it all.

Suddenly she turned on Laura like a cobra.

"What exactly do you mean that you regret what you did with Frank Patterson?" Bella asked with a sharp tone that had not been there before.

"Well that I, you know..." Laura stumbled uncertain what to say. Myself, I had always been curious as to what my wife did in Paterson's bedroom, but I was too much the coward to ask. Bella had none of my inhibitions. As I watched in horror and with growing disgust, Bella began to pry the details from Laura. She would accept no euphemisms. The more Laura tried to evade, the more Bella zeroed in. I will admit sympathy for my wife, as much as I hate what she did, it was clear that, however enjoyable the experience might have been at the time, now it was a deep abiding wound.

Bella went on from there to expose Laura's sexual history prior to our marriage. She never used the words, but she implied Laura was a common slut. A picture of Laura began to emerge. She was not who I though she was. The woman I knew was sure confident and a little condescending. This Laura was insecure. She was unsure of her looks and felt men only wanted her for sex. It was shocking, but I believed it because the Laura I thought I knew would never admit to being less than in control.

Laura's face was covered in a sheet of tears. It had always amazed me how her nose ran like a faucet when she was deeply upset. Laura was huddled in her chair, tears running down to drip from her chin and her nose, snot running down over her lips- there were not enough tissues in the world to contain the flow. After what seemed like an eternity it was done, I had stopped listening, it was too painful. When I looked at my watch, it was 1:30 p.m. I had missed my train.

"No problem. Laura can't drive herself back north in her condition anyway. You will need to drive," Bella said as light and cheerful as if we had been discussing gardening for the last one-hundred-twenty minutes.

As I helped Laura up and out, Bella gave a cheery, "See you two next week."

Laura's eyes searched mine, at one point I saw fear in them. I am sure mine were, at worst, showing my confusion. This was her counselor and I had no idea why Bella had so thoroughly crushed and humiliated Laura.

It took some time to find Laura's car in the parking garage that was two streets over. I got her into the passenger side of the BMW convertible that I knew so well. I drove a five year old Honda Civic that Laura had purchased for me new. Her eighty thousand dollar sports car we bought three years back when we moved to Albany, a kind of going away present for both of us, although I never drove it preferring the Honda. I guess I am not what is considered a macho man, I hate cars.

As a kid growing up in a middle-class Brooklyn neighborhood no one had a car, for one thing we had no place to park them. Our lives revolved around subways and busses.

The BMW was almost paid for. She loved this stupid car I thought as I helped her into it. I did not want Laura's car, I thought about trying to deprive her of it, but it was just too expensive to maintain and I hated to even look at it. To her it was a status symbol. It said that she was an important lawyer. On some level the car pissed me off. Now I knew it was more than a status object it was a crutch for her week self-esteem.

The drive back to Albany was quiet. I had trouble in the first part getting out of the City, for someone born and raised there I never drove there. I was in sticker shock for the parking fee which was nearly as much as my round-trip train ticket. Laura was curled up almost comatose in the passenger seat. About Newburg she began quietly to sob. I don't know why but I put my hand on her shoulder and gave a squeeze. This brought on a crying fit.

"Laura please it's over now. Please sit up and stop crying."

"You don't know how I miss touching you. It sounds so stupid, but sometimes I just need to touch you," she said.

I had no come back to that.

"I miss the way you looked at me. I know you hate me now and don't even want to see me, but I miss you so much," she said, followed by more tears and the sobs were no longer quiet.

When we reached Selkirk, I asked her where I was taking her, that's how I found out she was staying with Susan and Steven or more accurately in Susan's house that she shared with Steven. However, he was not currently in residence being out of town defending a spouse who had clearly killed her husband.

When we reached Becher Road in Altamont, the pleasant times we use to have taking this drive came back to me. When I saw that the long drive up the little hill from the road to Susan's house was now paved I realized it had been some time since I visited here. It had been an old farm house once, a dinky little thing, now it was a six bedroom house with a free standing four bay garage and a rustic barn out back that they intended one day to turn into an office when Susan started having babies and Steven would become a stay-at-home Dad, working part-time out of the house. I wondered how that plan now squared with his sudden notoriety as a defense counsel.

I pulled the Beemer to a stop at the garage.

Laura turned to me and said, "I never loved anyone before you. I am so sorry. You probably will never forgive me, but please try to remember the good times we had." Then she raced from the car over the flag stone walk, over the big farmhouse porch, and into the house. I got out closed the doors on the car as I did Susan came out of the house. The time was a little before four in the afternoon and I was surprised to see her home so early. She came down the porch steps to stand arms across her chest glaring at me. She wore jeans and a beat up Fordham University sweatshirt that must have been Stevens. She was still the most beautiful woman around.

"You proud of yourself Pat?" she said.

"Wasn't me, was the damn counselor."

"I see-you had nothing to do with this. You just get to go around acting like a child and nothing is your fault," Susan said.

There were nasty things I could have said back to her about her own conduct, but I bit my tongue. "Please Susan stay out of this."

"How can I? When two people that I love are being destroyed over nonsense."

"Isn't nonsense to me," I replied.

"So sure of yourself so strong. No tolerance for us weak individuals. I hope someday you and Steven learn what it is to be human." As she said that she turned and went back into the house.

OFFENCE AND JUSTICE

I called a cab on my cell phone as I walked down to the road. It took forty minutes to arrive, and I had time to curse Bella Moskowitz, Roxanne Clearmont and Angela Zink and all the other allegedly good women who I am convinced secretly hate men and make our lives miserable. I also had time to ponder Susan's last remark. What did it mean?

I did not have Night Court that night; call it the one privilege of my new position.

About midnight I got a call from Steven.

"Hi Pat, I would ask how things are going, but I know," he said.

"Yea. What did Susan tell you?"

"Well you are impossible, immature, insensitive, and probable insane and those are just the i-words. I got well over two hours of your faults on the phone," he said.

"Sorry, not your problem, I know you are on trial and don't need to hear about my shit."

"Not your fault either, besides it was a needed break."

"So how's it going?" I asked

"Could be better," Steven answered.

"That bad."

"Other side is not making many mistakes. She is good I will give her that."

"Just a her," I said.

Steven laughed and said, "She is the one that breaks the rule."

As a rule women make mediocre trial attorneys at best, something in the chromosomes I guess. They lean toward cooperation not conflict and a trial is just a fight, the dirtier and meaner you can play it the better. Give away nothing and hit from behind if you can. Trials don't appeal to most women, but there are exceptions.

"I just wish I was not playing with a handicap," he said.

"Oh, what's that?" I asked.

Steven hesitated then in a very low voice, he said. "The client is innocent."

I did not respond for a moment then all I could think of to say was "sorry."

"Not your fault these things happen," he said.

"Things all right between you and Susan," I asked.

"Ok, why you asking."

"Well, she said something funny when I saw her about you and me not being human," I said.

There was a long pause and then he said." I think she is having problems handling my success. Don't know for sure, but it's a hunch. Well I'll probably lose this one and things will go back to normal," he said.

We ended the call promising to meet when he got back for a drink.

Jenny Trudeu was a 'skinny ass white ho' or so she told me the first time we met.

We met because she had been arrested for soliciting, but the bust was questionable.

"I may be just a ho, Mr. Sullivan, but I know a cop when I see one. This charge is bullshit."

It was and I let it go and moved on. She was grateful then and I hoped she still was.

"So what you want Mr. Bigshot DA? Need my professional service. I hear things ain't good at home," she said.

CHAPTER SIX

Nothing goes unnoticed in this town and I was sure the rumors were flying since I filed for divorce.

"Need a favor of a different kind," I said.

"Well you can ask, but what you did for me on the bullshit charges before only comes natural to a good guy like you."

I pulled out a photo array. A set of pictures usually used to show a witness instead of a full line up to see if the witness can pick out the suspect. Only in this case, they were all suspects, members of the Vultures bike gang."

I saw the recognition in Jenny's eyes.

"You recognize these guys," I said.

"Yea and I sure don't owe you anything like that," she said.

"The DA needs your help and I guarantee it'll never come back on you."

It took me the better part of an hour to convince her but in the end she agreed. We then had to concoct the story. Most of it was true she had been in the Vultures' clubhouse providing her professional services. All we added were some overheard conversations to the effect that Samuel Tatro aka Tater, or when he wasn't around Tater Tot, was in possession of a machete.

"So that is our story and all you need to do is tell it to Sergeant Brandt and he will do the rest," I said, satisfied that we would soon have the search warrant we needed.

"I trust you Mr. Sullivan to take care of me," Jenny said.

I assured her that it would be all right. In truth, I was not that certain.

We found the machete in a storage locker in a rundown little town north of Albany called Watervliet. Following Tater had paid off. All we had to do now was get somebody to talk. I hauled Tater in and sat him in a room for twenty-three hours and charged him with weapons possession for the Machete. We next hauled in Little Tom aka Thomas Lexington a six foot five two hundred eight-five pound giant of a man. There was no way the five foot seven Tater had severed the head of Ricky St. Simon. I figured that honor went to little Tom.

By the time we started questioning Little Tom, he figured that Tater had ratted him out and he gave us what we needed to make the balance of the arrests. They hit on

Memorial Day weekend. I was just six weeks into my eight month term.

I knew how Russell Dewit, the Republican Chairman of Van Patten County, was thinking. The DA's office seemed like the kind of plum he would be able to squeeze some juice from. In a heavily republican county an unoccupied office was a present. The temporary guy, that Sullivan kid, had seemed to be no problem when he got in trouble with that headless corpse. Now he had made arrests and the same so-call journalists who were castigating him just last week were calling him the most capable DA in the State. Christ, he was going to have to go back and rethink his entire strategy. Run that fool Dexter Eling who was someone the public knew without actually knowing how incompetent he was. He would probably be able to run a better candidate next time. That gave me the opportunity to run against Dexter. I was looking forward to it.

By the end of August we had been going at the counseling for almost five months. It had been many weeks since the session where Bella had torn Laura apart. Bella had spent that time building Laura back up. Laura was almost the sure confident woman I had married again. I decided there was a method in Bella's madness. I could see Laura was on the verge of forgiving herself. Even I was grudgingly ready to forgive her. What I was not willing to do was stay married to her, as far as I was concerned my life with Laura was over.

"What's the matter Pat can't get past your pride?" Bella asked in our private session.

"No. It's that I can't get past the illusions I had. I guess I married too young. I was immature, the way some people say I am acting now. She was like a goddess to me. I guess I wasn't seeing clearly."

"Who really knows the person they marry. We wear masks out in the world. Marriage is partly about learning to love the other person as they are. Not as we wish they were. You may have been naïve, but you don't have to stay that way," she said.

"You're right, but it's time to grow up and move on as you've been preaching, but I intend to go forward without Laura."

Bella shook her head. "Well you're a real tough nut, I know there will come a day you'll regret what you're doing. You married Laura in the presence of God for better or worse. For you that's an eternal bond. You belong to her and God has a way of working her will so I'm going to leave this to God. I'll inform the Judge that the counseling will stop at the end of September until then I'll work on separating you two. Is that Ok with you?" She said turning those deep eyes of hers on me.

"Sounds good," I said.

She told us the same thing in the general session and Laura looked sad, but I thought she took the news well.

When I got out Brandt was waiting in a Sherriff's highway cruiser, I was getting escorted everywhere. The death threats started showing up just after the fourth of July. By early August the FBI was telling us to take them seriously. The Vultures had hired high price New York counsel and were fighting the indictments. Both Tater and Little Tom were trying to take back their confessions. The prominent City lawyers were claiming the evidence was tainted and should be suppressed. They were screaming illegal search when they were not talking about rural courts and white justice which meant hicks in white sheets.

When I got in the Sherriff's vehicle Sergeant Brandt handed me his cell phone. The text was from Phil Sloane. It was one word, "Geronimo!" Brandt was smiling like a kid at Christmas. The code word was not original but it was totally unbreakable. It meant that the other side had bought the deception. It was so simple a ploy I knew it would be effective.

About three weeks before we had obtained information the FBI was going to put one of the girlfriends of the Vultures in witness protection. Her name was Jasmine Turner. She was one of the few girls that hung with these black bikers who was herself black; she was also childless and looking for a new start in life. The Feds had turned her, unfortunately, as they told us she knew nothing about the St. Simon murder. No problem she had the right initials JT. Those were the initials of Jenny Trudeu, and were how Jenny was referred to in all our internal documents. Jenny's full name appeared nowhere. What we needed to do was convince everyone that JT stood for Jasmine Turner.

Phil, Jack Brandt, and I let the Feds sweep up Jasmine, and then begin a quiet but increasingly desperate search for her. Soon even the people in our office thought our informant was Jasmine Turner, and we could not find her. The Vultures' attorney thought they had it aced. The suppression hearing was set for the second Tuesday following Labor Day. I had a pass on counseling that day. But the Geronimo meant our real enemy had bought it. Dexter Eling had been running a hard-driving campaign to get the DA's office, that he thought by rights was his. We had found out he was due on the early morning local news hour next Sunday. We were hoping he would take a shot at me, convinced that I could not win the suppression hearing. Geronimo meant the reporter who was going to interview Dexter had been told to ask about the suppression hearing. Phil had a source at the TV station. We were going to let good old Dex walk right into it. However, we had better win that hearing.

"I want to sit second chair on the hearing," Mary Ellen Seamon announced from in front of the big desk, that I could never get use to. I was contemplating replacing it as soon as I won the election.

SIR PATRICK BIJOU

"I know you don't think much of my courtroom ability, but how can I improve if you don't give me a chance," she said.

She was right of course, I didn't think much of her ability, and she would not improve unless she got more experience. I also had come to respect her; she had guts and she didn't run away when I got the DA's job like the rest had. She deserved a chance.

"Alright you can, but it isn't a free ride. You have to prepare the witness and examine her."

"But we don't have a witness- I mean-do we?"

I smiled. "The first lesson here is learning how to deceive," I said.

Mary Ellen turned out to be perfect. She spent a week writing questions and preparing to examine a witness she was not allowed to meet. I gave her all the information and coached her on how to formulae the questions including preparing two or three different versions of each question just in case there was an objection and it was sustained. Then we went over and over it. Finally Mary Ellen was allowed to examine Jenny over a secure phone line. I wasn't taking any chances.

On the second Tuesday in September, the Van Patten Courthouse was sealed; only those who needed to be there were allowed in. Jenny was in the main Courtroom behind a screen where only the sitting Judge could actually see her. She had been smuggled into the Courthouse inside a trunk and that is how she would go back out.

Judge Drego was on the bench, and was wearing a surprised look as the New York attorney's entered. Jenny was behind the thick screen.

"Your honor, we protest this arrangement. We have a right to confront the witness. He or she should not be allowed to hide their identity behind a screen," began Thomas Jacobson, chief defense counsel for Percy Jackson aka PJack.

"Mr. Sullivan?" the judge asked.

"Your honor, this is an anonymous witness for good reason. These are violent men who decapitate their victims. Our witness will be identified for these proceeding as Ms. Jane Rowe, but we will of course reveal her actually identify to your Honor."

"How is anyone to know that you have been given her true name judge, or that she is not some government plant?" Jacobson demanded. Before I could reply the Judge spoke.

"Mr. Jacobson, I know the lady. In fact, I've known her since she was a little girl. I do not need the DA to tell me who she is, and now if you don't have a further objection we will take her testimony."

SIR PATRICK BIJOU

"Mr. Sullivan you may begin," the judge said

I leaned over and whispered to Mary Ellen, "Go to it girl."

There are three things you need to win a case- Preparation, Preparation, and Luck. That day we had all three. Mary Ellen was certainly prepared, and she believed in every lie that Jenny told. We two, that is Jenny and I, had done a good job of building a false story on a structure of truth until the falsehood had become inseparable from the truth. Mary Ellen just added an element of believability. She was nervous and inexperienced and the fact I let her take the lead said I was completely sure of my case. Mary Ellen brought out Jenny's occupation on direct. Judge Drego just shook his head and asked.

"What would your parents think, Ms. Rowe?"

"Judge you know my husband died and left me with the two boys. The social security and that little bit of Workers Comp just ain't enough," Jenny replied reminding Drego of the industrial accident that had killed two and injured six others. All had been former General Electric workers. When GE pulled out, it had farmed a process to a small company started just for that purpose. The new firm did not have the insurance benefits the bigger company had. The accident left Jenny a widow and she managed the best way she could. Odd hearing Jenny's justification made me think of Laura, had she made a similar choice of family over self-respect. Maybe she had, but with far less cause.

The coup de grace was given by the other side. Jacobson and each of the defense Counsel for all five defendants had their shot, but Jenny could not be budged.

Jacobson was up last and he was honing in on Jenny's character.

"Ms. Rowe, you tell us you overheard a conversation after completing work (smirk) and heading to the bathroom to clean up for further labors (smirk). You can't recall exactly, but you had serviced four or five men to that point. CORRECT?" Jacobson asked.

"Yes that is correct," Jenny replied.

"Well, Ms. Rowe, what does that make you?"

"Just what I told Mr. Sullivan the first time I met him, a skinny ass white ho," she replied.

Even Drego laughed and that is how the high powered attorney lost, because Jenny's version of the truth was now the truth.

When we exited the courthouse, all three local TV stations had their trucks waiting. I forced myself to smile and make humble appreciative statements thanking the judge and our courageous witness. We made the evening news, eleven o'clock news, and the following morning broadcasts. Dexter could not be reached for comment.

Money began coming in. I got a big contribution from Saul Solomon which I was sure was actually from Laura. I appreciated that, and Edward Kincade sent a very generous sum as did Steven. But these paled in compared to the one hundred thousand that a man I did not know from Vermont sent. Apparently his son died of a heroin overdose. It was his way of fighting back. There were many small contribution twenty five dollars or less. I was amazed. Some came with notes praising my work or thanking me. I felt like a fraud. This had started with my anger over my wife's infidelity. Now people looked up to me for things that I was personally ashamed of. When I confessed this to Bella she just turned those eyes on me that looked right through you.

"As I said when we started, this ultimately comes back to you being able to accept what you've done. It doesn't matter what the world believes when you know the truth. Contrary to what you've been trying to sell to everyone including yourself, there is something we call truth that is not variable as the circumstances dictate."

Was she right, I no longer knew? I got caught up in the elections. It was a real fight. I am no politician. Going around glad handing people is the hardest thing for someone like me. It took all my will power to endure the endless interactions with people. To add to my problems Dexter got a real break from the Feds. They cut deals with the Vultures and whisked them off to protective custody. One headless corpse was worth less than the so-called important information they had on the drug trade. We tried to bargain for at least one body to prosecute, but apparently some deal had been made. The state Attorney General announced the deal at a press conference. It was either go along or try to take on the state. The Governor was nice enough to send me a thank you note.

Before I knew, it was the first Tuesday in November. Election Day dawned clear and bright, but it rained later in the day. As I got up that day I though back to where I was a year before. I was preparing for the Leroy Johnson trial. Odd I had not thought about him in a long time. He had gotten probation and I heard was back with his wife. I had beaten the rap and burned the bitch and I wondered who was happier.

I made the rounds of the polls that day. I was greeted with enthusiasm by all the poll workers, democrats and republicans. About noon I ran into Tommy LeCour. He thanked me for revitalizing the party.

"Can't thank you enough Pat. Win or lose we owe you, never seen the organization so up before," he said with a broad smile on his face.

Rumor had it that turnout was way up for an off-year election. Not a surprise. In the presidential election a little over twenty five thousand votes had been cast in the county as a whole. Dexter had raised and spent over One Hundred Seventy Five Thousand dollars. I had in fact out-spent him. Together we had spent almost fifteen dollars for every vote that would be cast. It was unheard of, but the republicans still had a two to one registration advantage.

It was just before six in the evening when I exited the last polling place. Brandt was with me, he was out of uniform as were about two dozen of his fellow officers who had been campaigning for me all day. He had gotten hung up talking to some people as we exited the Polish American Community Center where the 14th election district had its polling place. I came out into the street just as it was getting dark. I heard the motorcycle before I saw it, as I looked the rider had his helmet down and was roaring toward me. He had something in his right hand a bat or a small pole. It was obvious what he intended. I could run, but I was not going to escape. As he reached me, I heard the shot. The rider slumped the motorcycle went out of control. It nearly missed me, but the back wheel hit me and threw me against a parked car. The motorcycle came tumbling after.

The room was not quite dark; there was light coming from the hallway through the door and a big window into the outer room. I was in a bed and I seemed to be attached to every machine around me. Someone came in and leaned over the bed. A nurse I guess.

"Easy now don't try to move."

"He's awake," she said turning to someone who was apparently seated.

A figure rose up to stand beside the nurse. I did not need to see her to know who it was, Laura. They got me water to drink and made me stay still.

"Don't try to move. You need to rest, some things aren't quite working." This turned out to be an understatement. I had the impact injuries and apparently my head injury had resulted in a stroke.

But I was in the hospital by then and the stroke was not terrible. My right arm was broken, my left arm partially paralyzed along with my left leg. My head felt as if a hammer had been taken to it, but mostly I just hurt. The doctors and nurses were upbeat and positive predicting an almost full recovery, but almost covered a lot. A very pretty female psychiatrist began visiting me on my third day in the hospital. She did not use the word, but crippled was definitely what I saw in her eyes.

"It'll take time and a lot of work on your part," said the lead doctor whose name I never quite caught.

Laura was there with me and there was no getting rid of her, what I wanted was ignored. She took over, talked to the doctors, and insisted on having things her way. One of my nurses turned out to be the recent graduate Kathy Lumious. Apparently she convinced the security that she was on my side now. She was very nice and thanked me for getting rid of the big black fucker so that she could get on with her life.

"By the way he's not you know."

"What?"

"Big, least not down there. Either that black thing is all myth or he's the exception that proves the rule. But thank God he's gone. Those stupid Feds asked me, 'Did I want to go with him?' How dumb did they think I was?"

They sent me home on the sixth day with Laura. When I tried to point out to her that we were getting a divorce, she laughed at me.

"We had that nonsense dismissed," she said, "Who's going to take care of you if not me?"

If you are interested, I lost the election by less than two hundred votes. It was close, and the republicans lost seven seats in the county legislature and a majority of the town councils. Dexter was happy in his victory until the news-people began asking him about the attempt on my life. The guy on the bike was dead, killed by Brandt who saw what was happening as he exited the Polish Community Center. He had simply dropped to one knee and took the guy out. However, the public wanted more blood. The editorials all bemoaned the lack of progress on the case in Van Patten. "Will the drug trade return to Van Patten now that Sullivan is gone?" apparently the news hounds were sure it would and that soon the sky would also fall in as well.

Laura did her best to isolate me from everything. She had to return to work the third week I was home. She had arranged for a male nurse/physical therapist named Donald. She converted the family room into a physical therapy room. Don worked with me relentlessly to get me back into physical shape. But he never lied to me; it was never all going to come back. I would walk maybe even fast, but not run. I would probably need a cane or crutch but not a walker. I could use my arms with some difficulty that would hopefully pass in time. Don was determined and so was I.

I swore to Laura that as soon as I was able I would restart the divorce. Even to me it sounded like so much wishful thinking. I had a good way to go. About four weeks after my release from the hospital Laura took me to see a new doctor. I had not had a regular physician. Elizabeth Harper was a family practitioner or at least that is what the sign said. She examined me and said I was making good progress and she complemented Nurse Donald Pleasant, Jr. for his efforts.

"Don is the best and you are doing fine Mr. Sullivan," Dr. Harper said, but mostly she spoke to Laura about what was needed.

Finally with a wink she said, "I think that you're ready to make your wife happy again."

I got the drift as Laura began to blush.

Laura was very affectionate all the way home, but I tried to keep her at a distance. It was difficult, and I was horny as hell. I had been able to control my urges when I had been running a DA's office and trying to run for office, but now I had time to think of sex and no alone time between Don and Laura. I have said that I loved Laura. But I have not been entirely honest about Laura. She is not the classic beauty that Susan Singleton Fitzgerald is, but she has far more sexual attraction. I cannot explain it, but while Susan will turn every head in a room when she enters, for some reason Laura will make every man into a satyr. She has this appeal that goes directly to your libido. In actuality, I am more immune that the average man, but when she wants to turn up the heat, I am helpless.

That night she appeared in my room in a silky black teddy, it had been nearly a year and I was not up to resisting. Moreover, she made it all about me. She started with a blow job strait from heaven. I frankly did not know she had that kind of talent. She is a woman who on the hottest day in July has hands so cold that you would believe she was made of ice. However, her vagina, cunt, pussy or whatever you want to call it is an oven. It clearly sucks all the heat from the rest of her body.

I had broken bones and was partially paralyzed but I had a fully functional cock. She had me tall and hard just walking into the room. She laughed as she slipped me into her cunt having brought me to the edge with her mouth.

"So are you going to hold out as usual? I think not, it's been too long. No forty minutes this time," she said. She was right she took me and just kept laughing.

"You know I love the way you come and just stay hard," she said continuing to ride me cowgirl. She kept fucking me until I came again. She seemed to be on a mission. After I came the third time I asked the question I had asked before. It seemed to have been a life time ago, that evening in Connecticut.

"Are we protected?" I asked.

Her laugh was deep and nearly hysterical.

"Why should I take precautions? I'm fucking my husband and I'm a junior, soon to be a senior partner, time to start a family," she said.

Three weeks later she showed me the test stick with its little blue plus sign.

"Sorry Pat, you lose, but then you really didn't think you would win did you?" Laura said.

But it was not over yet, there were more cards in play.

CHAPTER SEVEN

The Hudson River flowed majestically toward New York Harbor. The view from the tall west side office building's 44th floor was breathtaking as Edward Kincade, Governor of New York, looked out his office widow and considered the ancient waterway. The Hudson was shaped by the glacial melt-off over ten-thousand years before. As a river, it was more a finger of the ocean. The ocean tide reached north as far as and sometimes farther than Poughkeepsie, a city midway up the river valley. Now with the rise of sea level the ocean and river threatened the lives and welfare of the millions who lived and worked in the great city below the Governor's office. Kincade had envisioned himself as the savior of his city, but as always his reach exceeded his grasp.

On this Sunday he was in his office attended by the four most powerful men in state government. The Speaker of the State Assembly, the Majority Leader of the State Senate, the Attorney General and the verbose and pompous Harvey Millhouse, Chief Judge of the New York Court of Appeals, the oddly named highest state judicial body. The topic that brought these powerful men together was the latest fuck up.

Harvey was explaining in his most boring fashion why the Court could not state in advance that the particular piece of legislation was unconstitutional, in other words why he would not stick his neck out to save the party and in particular the Governor from looking both foolish and hypocritical. The Governor had taken Harvey's class on torts at Harvard and he had been just as boring there, if somewhat more useful.

"Ok, Harvey we get it. We're 'hoisted on our own petard' and you're not going to help us get down," Speaker Stanley Schwartz said.

"Well I just can't," Harvey responded.

"It's all my fault," Paul Devenback, Senate Majority Leader said.

"Stop beating yourself up Paulie these things happen. The Republicans have been in charge so long in your house that you guys are out of practice," the Speaker said.

For years the Republicans held a slim majority in the state senate under a deal that allowed the upper house to be gerrymandered Republican while the lower house was gerrymandered Democrat. It mattered not which party the votes favored in any particular election. The parties found mutual benefit in their deal which assured power in at least one house of government to each party no matter how the voters were inclined.

SIR PATRICK BIJOU

When State Senator Mark Hoffman brought his wife of twenty-seven years to the Mercy General emergency room one night, beaten and bleeding, she claimed to have fallen down the stairs. The hospital personnel did not believe her and reported the abuse. Nothing happened! The DA was the Senator's brother.

The Republican State Senate had passed a special bill to appoint an independent prosecutor to investigate the incident. Hoffman was in fact one of the few upstate democrats in the state senate. The Assembly responded under the shrew leadership of Stanley Schwartz, veteran of some of the bitterest and dirtiest battles in Brooklyn Clubhouse politics.

The Assembly Bill called for the appointment of a special prosecutor to investigate state elected officials, a Corruption Czar. You would have to be a fool to vote for such a bill. Therefore, each house had passed a bill. The Democrat Assembly could say they passed a bill to investigate and the Republicans refused to sign it. The Republicans could claim the Democrat bill was a sham. Everything was fine until Sherry Smith finally succumbed to breast cancer.

In Stanley's view Sherry was a great dame. She was a Republican but he always got along with the overweight black woman who he kidded about her weight and who gave it right back to him. She was good on women's issues and minority rights, but incredibly conservative. She held a gerrymandered district in Buffalo by force of personality. It should have swung the other way but she wouldn't let it. She fought the cancer just as hard but lost.

Then there was that prick Pleasly, Franklin (not frank) Pleasly was a self-righteous SOB who got elected solely on holding the most heavily Republican seat in either house. He died in a whorehouse of a heart attack although that location was never reported in the press. His death meant two special elections. But no sweat the most the Republicans could lose was one.

Taking no chances, a conservative Christian mother of three boys was nominated to succeed Pleasly. She was early forties, slim, brunette, and attractively put together. No raving beauty, but very good looking and articulate. The pundits said Sara Monk, the wife of Dr. Monk an oral surgeon, couldn't lose. Unfortunately she did.

Sara was a stay at home mom who had backed conservative causes both financially with her husband's money and by being a dedicated campaign volunteer. She had been elected to the local school board and the town council. It was in this last job that she met a much younger attorney and began a brief liaison. It was minor and was over, but unfortunately in the age of cellular phones and selfies the pictures still existed.

Three days before the special election Sara Monk's nude and suggestive photos were all over the net. The scandal broke too close to the election for damage control, and the last shoe to drop was the boyfriend's ex-wife saying that Sara was the cause of the divorce. In a less conservative district, it might not have mattered so much.

The democrats were ecstatic when they took control of the State Senate. This lasted one whole day. The outgoing majority leader brought the assembly's version of the special counsel bill to the floor and then sat down. If Paul Devenback had been more experienced, he could have held his side together and thumbed his nose at the opposition, but he wasn't.

The radical left on his side of the chamber knew what they wanted: payback. What better way to get it than pass a radical reform bill. The best Paul could do was amending the bill to limit the term to five years. So there it was a bill no sane politician wanted sitting waiting for the Governor's signature. A bill he had endorsed when he was sure it would not pass.

The last man in the room was Sydney (Sid) Levy, the Attorney General, in New York an elected position. How Sid, the most honest and caring man that the others had ever known, was even nominated was a mystery, but here he sat with four political sharks. Sid was thirty five, the father of six, and husband of Ruth, an orthodox Jewish woman who believed in her faith to the exclusion of everything except her family. The meeting was on Sunday because the day before had been the Sabbath. Sid would have come the day before, but the others knew what a price Ruth would make him pay.

OFFENCE AND JUSTICE

"Well, Attorney General any advice?" the Governor asked.

Sid had been dreading this moment. He was uncomfortable with these men at the best of times. Now he was asked to give an opinion that he believed they could not agree with.

"Well the bill has certain deficiencies which could be corrected by the right appointment:

1. It is too general; it does not give a clear mandate, which means you need a strong person to fill the position.

2. There is no money appropriated which means until the next budget or the supplemental if there is one, this person must operate without funds. I will of course provide what assistance I can for support, but I cannot hire personal for another agency. So you need someone who is innovative.

3. Finally you need someone independent, that the public will respect, but who will understand human frailty. Not someone holier than thou, but still-I don't know-I guess hero enough for the public to look up to.

My opinion is: If you have someone like that, sign the bill and appoint him or her, but if you can't find the right person, veto it and take the bad press."

Sydney finished his statement to a groan from the Majority Leader and the Judge clearing his throat. The

Governor was oddly quiet. Then Stanley said, "Got someone like that in your back pocket, Ed?"

The Governor looked down then turned back to the window watched the Hudson for a minute then picked up the phone.

"Betty get me Don Pleasant, Jr., not Sr.—Jr." He then turned back to the others and said, "Why don't we refill our coffee cups while we wait."

The Governor had placed his head of security's son into a position to keep him informed on Patrick Sullivan. Better safe than sorry. The moment he heard of the attack he had wondered. The more he learned, the surer he was that the situation needed to be carefully watched. His own involvement was minimal, and the situation was stable for now.

The phone buzzed and Betty said, "I have Don Jr. on the phone."

"Don, how is the family?" the Governor began.

"All good Governor, what can I do for you this fine Sunday afternoon?" Don replied.

"Well I was wondering about your patient."

"I've several, but I assume you mean Mr. Sullivan. He's on the mend, he'll never completely recover, but in a few months he should be eighty percent."

"How about now, can he work?"

"Well he is a lawyer, not very physically stressful, but it would be wise to wait."

"If I can't?" Edward asked in a way that said he wouldn't

"He should be alright and it could even help him mentally." Don knew he was rolling over, but you don't turn down a Governor unless you are absolutely sure, and he wasn't.

"Thanks Don, give my regards to your partner," Kincade said hanging up. The others mostly looked at him, but not Stanley.

"You sure of Sullivan, Governor?" the Speaker asked.

"Yes."

"Who's Sullivan? I've never heard of him," the Judge asked.

"Patrick Sullivan, former interim DA of Van Patten County, is everything our Attorney General wants including the hero part," said Governor Kincade.

"He's not Ivy League, Judge," said Stanley Schwartz of City College and sure the Judge looked down on him because of that.

In the end they all agreed, the Governor would sign the bill and then immediately appoint Patrick Sullivan. The Governor's only concern was one he did not express, he was sure that if that problem came up it would be taken care of. This was the big game now and small problems were eliminated.

*****

"Fuck Me-Fuck ME-Oh-Oh-Oh—Yes—I'm coming!" Linda Segal was hugging the oversized pillow on the king size bed in the Hilton Midtown, suite of Steven Fitzgerald. The Westchester County ADA had her head down and her ass sticking up as Steve fucked her from behind. In the last three days they had explored many positions, but this was her favorite.

The current session had started Sunday evening at a little after ten p.m. They had gone out to a fancy pizza restaurant where cracker thin pies were served. The food had been OK, the sex after was world class. In three days Steven had licked her, fucked her, and driven her wild. Right now he had slowed down; but not stopped. Her thigh had begun to vibrate again with another orgasm that did not quite quit.

"Please Steven no more, you win—I give up," she said.

Steven pulled out, slapping her on the rump, "Ok but I'm not done yet," he said.

Linda rolled over on her back. She had not had a lot of lovers. She was no slut. Steve was her fourth. He was not like what had come before. It was not slam bang thank you ma'am or try to pound you into the bed, hope you come before I do. He was oh so slow to start and lots of licking all the right places and then loving you crazy. In the end, he had his cock zipping in and out of her pussy at a phenomenal rate.

"How do you do that?" she asked.

"Do what?"

"Last so long?" she said hitting him with the pillow.

"Can't tell you trade secrets," he said.

At that moment, she looked over at the clock. "OMG it's after four," she said.

Hopping out of bed she made a dash for the bathroom.

"Where are you going?" he asked.

"It's four-seventeen Monday morning. I have Court at nine-thirty and I need to be at the office at eight."

"Why not call in sick," he shouted over the running shower.

"NO CAN DO!"

She was out of the shower, teeth brushed, and climbing into her clothing in ten minutes.

"When will I see you again," he asked.

Lynda turned to him, placed her hand on his cheek.

"You know this is just sex—really great sex, but just sex," she said.

Taking her hand from his cheek, he kissed the palm of her hand.

"You sure there's nothing more Lin?" he asked.

"Oh, Steve we've been together four times now. We must've fucked for the better part of eight days. I've had more sex with you than I did in a year long relationship with my last boyfriend. But if you don't count the shop talk about evidence, murder, guilt, and innocence we haven't spoken a hundred words to each other. It's all sex," she said, sadness in her tone.

"Ok Mighty Mouse, I get it. Don't get serious," he said.

"Hey you know I hate that nick name, you trying to piss me off?"

Lynda was four foot nine, petite and exceedingly cute rather than beautiful. She weighed a good bit less than a hundred pounds and she keeps her long auburn hair up in a school teacher's bun most of the time. It was down now and she looked highly erotic. They called her Mighty Mouse because she was a human-dynamo and a highly aggressive trial lawyer.

To compensate for her height, she never wore heels less than six inches, a remarkable bit of endurance for a person whose life required running to and between courtrooms. But while it made her incredibly sexy and she charmed judges and opposing counsel, Steven had seen her shoes for what they were: the equivalent of a tell at a poker table. She was unsure of herself and the tough front she put on was surface thin concealing a soft interior.

Women lawyers he thought. They over compensate for every real and perceived flaw. They think they have to be sure, cool, and tough with so much effort expended in the appearance the substance has to be neglected. His best friend Pat Sullivan's wife was the perfect example of this on first appearance she was the picture of the self assured corporate attorney, but Steve knew better. Laura Sullivan was desperate to have people think the best of her. So greedy for success and approval that she was bound to fail. A weak woman married to a very strong man. Laura's husband was his friend—there could never be any question of that. They were brothers in all but blood. But and it was a big but Patrick was a wolf with a very dangerous bite and no real weakness except for an over protective character.

Steve knew he was more calculating and far less empathic than his friend Pat and, therefore, stronger than Pat but he had a weakness actually lots of them. They came in all sizes, but only one sex and he was helpless to resist. Someday he knew his love of women would bring him down. He would meet that one who was truly strong and she would take him out. All his tricks and skills would be useless when faced with a sure strong woman. He feared no man, but he had this nagging feeling that out there was one person of the opposite sex he could not deceive, but who could deceive him.

Lynda was not that woman. When she first heard that Carolyn Wellesley, who was accused of killing her husband Arthur Hale Wellesley, had switched attorneys to some upstate whiz kid, she immediately set out to research the new opposing counsel. What Lynda learned made her more than leery.

Foxy Fitzgerald was exactly what his nick name implied if the accounts were to be believed. She had no intention of underestimating him or giving him a shot at her back. He was untrustworthy and she was not about to be deceived. She had the home Court advantage and she used it well. The judge and the press were on her side and she took full advantage every chance she got. But near the end of the trial she began to sweat. He was just too good, she had expected tricks. What she got was a well laid out case for suicide. In the end, the Jury either agreed with Foxy or could not disagree.

OFFENCE AND JUSTICE

At first, she took the acquittal hard. During the trial, she had developed some physical attraction for her very pretty opposing counsel. How she wondered could a man be so pretty and still be straight. She decided to seduce him both to scratch the itch that had developed and to trap him into admitting the guilt of his client. The sex was great-he was something exceptional in bed. He had this incredible staying power and a very rapid recovery. However, when she used her feminine wiles to try to wheedle the truth from him she hit a very odd reaction.

Lynda was a sharp prosecutor, maybe not in Steven's league, but she could see the evasions he made. It was a little before they parted the morning after a wild night of sex that the gestalt hit.

"OMG! she was innocent," she said. The evidence adding up now that she saw what was being held back.

"If she had the note why didn't you use it?" But of course, he didn't answer he couldn't. But she knew there was a note and it contained something the wife did not want anyone to know about her husband. Carolyn Wellesley protected her husband even after his death. This profoundly affected Lynda. The hard driving prosecutor had a big soft spot and Steven Fitzgerald knew it.

"Alright Lin I will not call you Might Mouse although you may call me Foxy, and you are right, I'm a lousy companion—I am introspective and boring because I am all about my work. I am shit as a husband and don't see if I would be any better as a father. So answer my question when can I see you again?" he said.

"How about next weekend at my place?" she said.

He gave her a kiss and they parted. Lynda on the long drive back to Westchester wondered about his wife. She was getting the crap end of this. She had the moody quiet husband, but not the great sex. Supposedly she had a boyfriend but that must be like eating beef jerky when you could have filet mignon. Well, so much the better for me she thought.

*****

"He's fucking that midget," Susan said.

"Susan isn't that part of the deal in an open marriage?" Laura asked.

"Who said anything about an open marriage? Really Laura!" Susan said.

They were sitting in the Illium Café in Troy, an upscale sort of place that was good for lunch or breakfast. It was Thursday morning and they had feta cheese and spinach omelets in front of them. Laura was making a special effort to eat the fruit served with the omelets. Being five months pregnant she was trying to be good. It was not easy for her. She was sick a lot and extremely depressed.

"Susan when you step outside the lines you open yourself up," Laura said.

"Speak for yourself. I don't buy this tit-for-tat thing. For starters men can't keep up their end. Steven never had to go wanting for sex. The thing I want most after fucking someone else is to go to bed with Steven. I need his sweet loving after. Can he say the same?- No! No! No!-It's every weekend she has my man. I can't even enjoy being with Tony, all I can think about is what that tramp is doing with my husband."

"I'm sorry Susan, I just think you gave a man with the morals of an alley cat a big get out of jail free card," Laura said.

"What about the card you gave Pat?" Susan said.

"You think I don't worry. Since the Governor appointed him special prosecutor I've done nothing but worry.

"That AG office is loaded with female barracuda. And that secretary of his, the only way she could show more skin would be to walk into the office naked," Laura said before going on.

"If only he stilled loved me," Laura said the tears beginning to flow.

"I'm sure Pat still loves you," Susan said without much conviction.

SIR PATRICK BIJOU

"We made love the other night." Laura said sadness in her tone.

"See I told you. It's just that he's a male and needs some time to get past his pride," Susan said.

"No it was pity sex. I was cooking diner. I had opened the canned peas and had them heating on low. I had made the instant mash potatoes- that's the hard part. Then I put the steaks in the broiler," Laura said and began to cry.

"Hey what's the matter?"

"I set the stove on fire. The grease from the steaks caught fire. Pat had to come and put it out," she said getting control of her tears.

"Why are you trying to cook?"

"I am trying to be a good wife. I guess- I got hysterical. He held me and told me it would be alright and then we made love. I came the moment he entered me. It is so much more intense now -well at least for me it is," Laura said then she looked hard at her friend.

"I need to tell you something. Pat has a juvenile record. He nearly beat a man to death," Laura told Susan.

"How did you find that out?"

"I was at the legislative office building when I ran into an old law school friend who works there. It was during the time they were reviewing Pat's appointment. Well we had lunch and she asked me about it. I pretended I knew and told her it was nothing. Later I asked Mr. Solomon, he said not to worry, Pat had been young and provoked." Laura was looking guiltily at Susan as she finished.

Susan understood. "It turns you on. With everything, Pat has done and proof of his violent nature, you're a bit afraid of him and that's exciting." As Susan said this Laura nodded.

"So?"

"Well I use to take him so much for granted, now it's like living on the edge of a volcano. I should hate it, but I don't, it's really sexy." Laura tried to smile at this.

Then a thought struck Susan, her husband must have known, but never said anything.

*****

Philip Sloane was in the Halfway Diner. He had no idea if it was actually halfway between any two places. Two weeks before he had been hired by the State's newest special prosecutor as a consultant. It had taken the newly elected DA of Van Patten County three days to fire Phil. It was surprising that it had taken that long. Phil had been promoted to chief investigator in VanPatten County by Patrick Sullivan. When Sullivan lost the election Sloane as Sullivan's appointee was a marked man. He possibly could have filed a Civil Service complaint, but all he wanted was a few more years of service before he retired. Better to look elsewhere. He was sixty-two he didn't have time to play with fools.

He had gone to see Pat Sullivan to warn him about the federal investigation. The attack on Sullivan was not gang related-any fool could see that. The assailant who was killed, by then Sergeant now Lieutenant, Jack Brandt was not black nor a member of a biker gang. He was a Dartmouth graduate down on his luck due to a taste for cocaine and a gambling habit. The fact that the man died solvent said it all if you knew the facts.

Sloane had gone to an AHH hockey game at the Knickerbocker Arena with an old friend in the US attorney's office. They had been invited to sit in one of the VIP boxes. Sloan was not surprised when members of the local FBI office just happened to be invited as well.

The agents began with innocent innocuous questions, but they were clearly fishing very close to the right pond. Phil was a master of the art being practice on him. He soon learned everything they knew and was misdirecting them away from the truth. Sloane felt he owed Sullivan at least a heads up. Two days later he casually dropped by the Justice Building in the Empire State Plaza Complex. What the locals called the South Mall a confusing description since there was no North Mall and the entire collection of building resembled as one critic had sagely said "a Mausoleum built by space aliens."

Squeezed into the back of the Justice Building's second floor were three little rooms which now housed the Office of the Special Prosecutor for Official Integrity and Standards. A small sign marked the end of the corridor housing the clerical personal of the State Attorney General's office and the beginning of the small domain now referred to as SPOIS.

Sloane was greeted by Sullivan's secretary Katrina, a pretty very young Hispanic girl, who had followed Sullivan for the Van Patten DA's office. Sloane noticed that she was dress to kill. She quickly and without fanfare showed Sloane in to the head man's little office. Sloane didn't wait to be asked his business or to pass idle small talk he lunched right in to what he knew of the FBI investigation.

Sullivan was an emotionless SOB with a pair of brass balls; he heard Phil out then immediately made his recruiting pitch. He wanted Sloane to work for him. Sullivan made it very clear he was not going to accept a no answer.

"So I get a contract as an independent contractor. I perform work and hopefully get paid in sixty days. I lose my unemployment, get no credit toward retirement and maybe don't get paid at all," Phil said.

"CORRECT," Sullivan said.

"Ok, when do I start?"

"Now I need you to go to Western New York and investigate the assault on Senator Hoffman's wife."

"Do I at least get travel money?"

"No, run an expense record, the AG will possibly reimburse you," Sullivan said.

So here Sloan was at half past eleven at night scrunched down on a seat in the last booth in the small diner waiting for the unsuspecting Elisabeth Duncan. The former Mrs. Federo was the managing nurse of the Mercy General Hospital, a small place that was suffering from the financial limitations placed on health care providers. Its main income came from the emergency services it supplied and general medical services to the Alton State Prison, a medium security women's facility.

Mercy was thirty miles from the next hospital and fifteen miles from the prison. It supplied needed services to the prison inmates and the local community that was significantly dependent on the facility. As head nurse of the ER, Beth as she was called, was principally responsible for the administration of those services.

Beth Duncan was an RN when twenty years ago her husband Ted Duncan was killed in an auto accident leaving her with three children and little insurance. She had worked hard and put all three through college. Her work ethic brought her to the top of her little pond at the hospital. Jason Federo was well aware of that.

Jay as he was known was a lothario. He sized Beth up pretty well as lonely and venerable with all the kids gone. She was married to him before she realized what he really was, but she was a strong women and soon was looking to divorce the lazy leach, but it cost her and put her right back in the single and alone category.

Beth set the assignments for the nurses. She was the kind of person who took the least desirable shift for herself. Three to eleven on Friday and Saturday nights was what no one wanted. She let another nurse get that off as she had no one who was looking to go out with her. She was fifty-nine and felt every year of it. Every Friday and Saturday she stopped for supper at the Halfway at the end of her shift.

Saturday night the Halfway was crowed there was no other place open for a long distance. Beth usually had to sit at the counter, but if there was a booth open, she took it. Phil was positioned so he could not be seen from the isle sitting in the booth, it looked open. Beth came in and headed straight for what looked like an open booth. Only as she began to sit down did she notice Phil.

"Sorry I didn't see you," she said getting back up.

"Please join me I don't need the whole table and I would welcome the company," he said. One of his strongest assets as an investigator was how harmless he looked. It took some work, but in the end she joined him. He asked about her job. She was wearing hospital scrubs. She told him what she did and he was suitably impressed.

"My job with the state is so dull," he said. He never said what he did. Soon he had her talking and had a date for Wednesday, her day off. He spent the next three weeks working on her. When he was not dating Beth he was bothering the staff at the state prison.

Janet Hoffman was employed, though not any longer, as a Correctional Services Counselor. She had seventeen years in that position and many friends at the Prison; they did not like talking to outsiders. They were a closed insular community, but that was their weakness, they knew everything there was to know about each other. It took a while, but he listened to what wasn't being said. When people don't want to tell you something bad enough you can tell. Sloane knew how to ask the innocent question that revealed the hidden subject. Dodge the question and you answered it.

It took a while, but Sloane learned all about the Rev. Jean Paul Belmount and Janet Hoffman. What he was missing was the last piece, the part Beth, who was in charge of the ER the Friday night Senator Hoffman brought his wife in, knew.

Beth was nervous and unsure of what to expect. She had taken Phil home with the expectation of taking him to bed, but at their age some consideration needed to be given to physical limitations. As they climbed the stairs toward her bedroom in her modest Cape Cod style house, she was worried about her sagging breasts and the extra weight around her hips. The wrinkles on her thighs, ass, and belly would hopefully go unnoticed if she kept the light low. But she was also excited for the first time in three years; she had a man to take to her bedroom.

"Phil," she said turning to him, "It's alright if you don't want to."

In reply he began to undress her, he was in no hurry. He kissed her lips and then the bare flesh as he uncovered it. He gently attacked her breasts as he slipped off her bra. He lay her down on the bed and removed her panties. He shed his own clothing and slid into bed beside her.

Beth felt the warmth of his body then the stiffness of his maleness as he cuddled and kissed her. He slowly let his lips descend as his fingers began to probe first her breasts and then between her legs. His touch was light tender unhurried. He was no boy she realized. He intends to take his time she thought, "How nice."

As his lips descended over her body she knew where he was going.

"You don't have to do that," she said.

"HUSH," he replied, it wasn't a request, but a command. She relaxed and let it happen.

Abruptly he was licking behind her knees and up her thighs. His hands were everywhere.

Phil reached her profusion of pubic hair and pulled it with his teeth; it hurt and aroused her. He brushed her labia and then encircled them with his tongue. Her first husband had gone down on her only twice and Federo not at all. What was happening was a new experience.

Phil was a master of his craft from long experience. He teased and withheld satisfaction. He watched her breathing and estimated her arousal. He intended to devastate her, leave her a limp quivering mass of flesh. It took forty plus minutes for her first orgasm, she was begging for release by then. When she was barely recovered, he began to fuck her. Two hours later they had done it all Missionary, Doggy, Cowgirl and positions she could not name. She lost track of her orgasms.

They lay cuddling together, she was exhausted and sleepy.

"Now did that make you forget that silly subpoena," Phil said.

"Oh why did you remind me," she said.

"Sorry, but as I said, it probably has nothing to do with you," Phil said, in fact he knew it did not. He had Sullivan issue it figuring she would turn to him for assistance and she did. His response was to take her out to a nice expensive dinner and then seduce her.

"But you don't know Phil, the only thing I can think of is that poor Hoffman family," she said with real pain in her voice.

"You mean the State Senator? What has he got to do with you?" he said knowing all too well.

"I was on duty the night his wife came in," she said.

"So what, it's just a wife abuse case, and the medical records are sealed. You have no problem do you?" he said.

For a moment she was silent.

"Maybe they want to know about the miscarriage," she said in a hushed whisper that he could barely hear.

"That poor family," she went on, "I don't want to be the one to hurt them."

"Maybe it was the Senator's," he prompted already knowing the answer.

"No, she asked if it was black, we couldn't tell, she was not far enough along, but she asked like she knew the answer," she said this and then fell into tears. Sloane comforted her, held her and told her it would all be alright and hated himself for his deceiving a good woman.

*****

SIR PATRICK BIJOU

Katrina came in and said that I had a visitor. She was wearing a skirt that was even shorter than usual and her blouse clung to her breasts in a most suggestive way. If she had a bra on in was shear and skimpy. I needed to have a talk with her.

"Mary Ellen wants to see you," she said

"Who?"

"Mary Ellen Seamon, we worked with her in the DA's office."

"Did she say what she wanted?" I asked and Katrina gave me that look that I was becoming familiar with that said I was an idiot.

"Mary Ellen how nice to see you," I said. She was wearing what I call the female lawyer uniform, a dark pin-striped skirt suit. It had a tight jacket that framed her breasts and a skirt that dropped to her knees. She wore three inch black and white pumps and black hose. She was, in other words, looking every bit the young female lawyer.

I showed her to a seat and waited. It took her a minute.

"I was hoping you had a job for me," she said.

I tried not to answer too fast.

"Sorry Mary, don't have a budget yet. No money to pay anyone."

"Kat is working here and I heard Sloane was," she said.

"Yes but they're not getting paid right now. They have contracts that say they get paid if and when we get a budget," I answered.

"Fine I'll take one of those," she said.

"But you're working; you have a job in Van Patten," I said.

"Right, I've a job but no career. I don't want to spend the rest of my life in traffic court, and I want to be a trial lawyer," she said.

"Be reasonable. You can go work and get paid elsewhere; here there's nothing, but a vague possibility."

"Your wrong, you're here and I want to learn. We worked well together when you were DA. I know you don't think much of me, but I'm here willing to work and I'm not going away. If I must, I'll hang out in the hallway until you hire me. Besides you need one woman in the office who's not trying to lure you into bed. I'm gay in case no one ever told you. I know you're too obtuse to have noticed on your own." She was stating her position and accepting no answer but yes. I'd not known about her sexual orientation but it made sense now that I considered.

"OK, you win, get a contract from Kat and start whenever you want."

She didn't realize it, but she had put the pressure on me. Now three people needed to be paid and it was certain there would be more. I needed a budget. The AG had been generous. He gave me temporary office space and spare equipment and office supplies. The independent contractor scam was an old trick to get around Civil Service, it allowed you to hire outside help for a limited period, but this was no substitute for a budget. When my staff put in their vouchers to be paid, I would need funds to pay them.

I needed a budget appropriation. I hated to do it, but I did not know where else to turn. I would need to eat my pride and put a good face on it. Being a politician was not what I had wanted out of life, but as my mother is fond of saying, "You don't get everything you want in this life."

His office was overly bright, the sun glared through the windows, but Saul Solomon did not seem to notice. We sat in two comfortable chairs; in addition there was a love seat and a coffee table. The coffee he was serving looked strong.

My mother also says that: the only thing worse than a poor loser was an ungracious winner, I had fought Saul Solomon and lost. I had come close to winning, but he had won the case. True he controlled the Judges, but I had known that going in. Where he really beat my friend

Steve and I was in his control of the Court Clerk. He took us off the Court calendar and kept us there. You can appeal a decision, but it's dam hard to appeal the lack of one. As a result I was married and likely to stay that way. The question I had now was Saul, a gracious winner?

"You take yours black no sugar I believe Mr. Sullivan," Solomon said handing me a china cup of the extra dark liquid.

"Yes thank you," I said. As I looked at the cup I was struck by the pink rose pattern. Rosenthal china like my Aunt Sophia had. He noticed me looking.

"I don't have many left they were my grandmothers. I enjoy having them here, a bit of a crutch to remind me where I come from," he said.

"Do you miss it?" I asked.

"Sometimes but what I miss is mostly gone. New York is a most unromantic place; it changes abruptly. Take yourself for example; a year ago you were someone entirely different a lowly ADA in a very small county, now you are the exalted State Special Counsel for Public Corruption. What you do from here on, good or bad, changes your life, those lives around you, and the lives of many you will never know," he reflected.

"Trouble is I have no budget," I said getting to what had brought me.

"Yes, but surely you've discussed this with the Governor," he said with a knowing smile.

"The Governor said when he told me of my appointment that he would include the office in his next budget, but until then, I'd need to depend on the AG. That just doesn't work. I need my own staff which means coming up with the money to pay them."

"Rather awkward situation asking the legislature to fund the person investigating them, particularly when it's someone they don't know, kind of an outsider," he said seeming to mull over the problem.

"I was wondering if you could give me any advice," I said getting back to what had brought me here and wondering how much he would twist me.

Saul smiled and then said: "What you need is a good lobbyist or two. I might know someone."

It was now my turn to smile, "Someone?"

"Pat you now have to think of yourself as an important man. Such men get what they want if they know how to ask for it. There will be a supplemental budget in July with lots of maneuvering and with the right help you could get some interim funding."

"So can you help me?" I asked, hating myself as I did it but realizing he was making it as easy as he could for me.

"Yes, I think I can. No promises, but if you retain this office to help you I will do everything I can." He said a smile on his face. He wasn't gloating, he was telling me he was pleased to have me as a client.

"I guess we better discuss fees then," I said.

"Mr. Sullivan I'm a lobbyist that's why you're hiring me. My job is to influence those who make the laws. There are many ways to do that, some are even legal," he said with a laugh.

"However, representing the man who will sort their dirty laundry and pass on their sins large and small, will say to them that I have influence where it counts. I'm not asking for any favors, just your gratitude," he said giving me a very sincere look. Then he continued, "As far as the firm is concerned I'll be doing a favor for the husband of one of our partners," he said this and leaned back.

"Well I can't argue with the price. Do we need a written retainer or will a handshake do."

"In this case, a handshake will do."

Saul was a gracious winner and if what people said was correct, someone who knew when to change sides.

Brandt came to see me. To put it succinctly he had been interviewed by the FBI, fortunately they had only asked about the evening of the attack on me. What he had seen and what he had done.

"I'm worried," he said, "no one with all the facts would believe that biker gang retaliation story. The guy I shot was no biker."

"Relax you've no part in any criminal activity. So long as you had no prior knowledge and took no action later to hide the activity, you're clear of it. The main thing to avoid now is a conspiracy charge," I said.

"That's easy to say, but just because I avoid indictment does not mean I'm clear. I'm high in the Sheriff's office now. When the current Sheriff retires I could run to replace him. If you are on the ticket, we could easily win. The worst case scenario I go out with a big pension. But all that goes to shit if that piss-ant talks."

It all came down to that. Everyone who knew or suspected Laura and Patterson's had an affair could point a finger. If you knew that I set him up and took that cheap bastard for the money that made me DA as retribution you could easily see what happened next. Patterson took his shot, but he only wounded me. It certainly was not over, but the FBI was now the wild card. If the Bureau learned of Laura's affair she and Patterson would come under suspicion for the attack on me.

OFFENCE AND JUSTICE

"That guy pissed himself the night I arrested him. He's not going to last five minutes facing an attempted murder charge. We need to do something," Brandt went on.

"No you stay out of this. Too many heads are on the line already."

The irony of a special prosecutor for corruption being caught in this situation was not lost on me. Something needed to be done. I was having trouble going there. The thing just kept escalating.

I hoped I had calmed Brandt down. I understood his concerns. This thing had started with his daughter in trouble, but now he had moved up and stood to move higher. It's hard to go back down because you get caught in a scandal brought on by a fool who doesn't know he was let off easy. His last words did not let me rest easy.

"You're not the only one I warned," he said.

Phil was in my office when I got back. He had it all written out in pencil on three sheets of yellow legal paper. I knew why it didn't go into a computer. Some of it was illegally obtained and that was the good stuff.

"Ok give me the material from the prison in an official report leave the rest out. I'll blanket the prison and the hospital with subpoenas. But we'll only need the wife and the Reverend in all probability to get an indictment. I figure Senator Hoffman will plead after that, once he knows that we know," I said to a very quiet Sloane. He had done a great job, but he did not look proud of himself.

"You Ok Phil?" I asked.

"Yea, just a case of guilt," he said and I did not probe into it.

Two days after I served the subpoena for Mrs. Hoffman to testify, I received an unexpected visitor. I had made arrangements to start presenting evidence to a Grand Jury. The AG had one seated for a commercial frauds case. I was borrowing this for my presentation of the Hoffman case. You can present anything you want to a grand jury so long as you have jurisdiction.

"Well, Steven what brings you here?" I said looking at my best friend.

"I represent Janet Hoffman," he said calmly as if he had asked me to lunch. Mary Ellen who was seated to my right taking notes near fell out of her chair. I asked her to observe as I did not want claims of favoritism later, but I had thought he was coming for the husband, the accused not the victim.

"Well, what can I do for your client," I asked.

"Quash your subpoena," he said. There was a force in his voice that said he was deadly serious.

"Sorry can't do that," I said.

"Then I'm here to tell you my client will invoke her Fifth Amendment rights," he said cool and matter of fact. I thought Mary would have apoplexy, but she kept her mouth shut.

"Fine I'll give her immunity," I said trying to be just as cool as her was.

In that case she'll invoke spousal privilege," he said, an unbidden smile cracking his face. He was clearly enjoying this.

It was too much for Mary she broke in. "You can't invoke spousal privilege for a crime against the spouse," she said with a decided smirk at her textbook evidence law.

"That's enough Mary," I said giving her a frosty stare and then I turned to Steven, "thank you for the heads up counselor—I appreciate the warning," I said.

"My pleasure Pat, after all we're friends," he said.

After he left Mary was apologetic for her outburst, but adamant that Steven was bluffing.

"I think not. He was delivering a message," I said.

"Ok I'll bite, what was the message?" she asked.

"That's the riddle; let's see if we can solve it. You go over Slone's official report and I'll search his notes."

SIR PATRICK BIJOU

*****

The next day I had nothing but a bad feeling that I had missed something crucial and a wife who was climbing the walls as the FBI began talking to people at her office. She was a suspect of course we had been in a divorce action until I was almost ridden down. They were clearly not convinced that drug dealers were after me.

"This is completely my fault," Laura said that night over the spaghetti dinner I cooked. I had strictly forbidden her to enter the kitchen. She was not even allowed to make coffee or boil water. She lit the stove up cooking steaks. Burned out the microwave with baked potatoes and managed to destroy a five hundred dollar fancy Cuisinart food processor from William Sonoma. The last I could not even figure out. We were having spaghetti because she had a craving for it.

She is normally useless in the kitchen but since the pregnancy she is positively dangerous. With the exception of her legal work she seemed to walk around in a perpetual fog. How she managed at the office was a mystery to me, but Saul assured me she was fine there.

After each doctor's visit, her OBGYN called me to complain that I needed to take better care of my wife. Her pregnancy was not easy in any respect. She was constantly horny and alternately sick. I defied anyone to get over with a very pregnant woman who orgasms almost as soon as you touch her. The sex was frustrating on my side and I was still a long way from getting past what she had done with Patterson. We were together in an uneasy relationship that I meant to end after the birth, hopefully with her consent to the inevitable.

"It's only partly your fault and as much as I hate to admit this you're the least responsible party involved," I said.

She calmed down a bit with that. She wasn't looking all well. I wanted to hire household help, but she refused, and I was broke. She was not sharing her money with me. I knew she was desperately afraid I would leave her given the chance and the funding. It was a problematic situation all around.

"What do I do if the FBI wants to talk to me," she asked.

"You tell them no, that they can put any questions in writing and you will answer them in writing after you speak to your lawyer."

"But that'll make me appear guilty," she said.

"Laura you are guilty. You had an affair. You stood by and let your husband extort your lover. Then you kept silent when your lover tried to murder your husband," I said.

"That's not true, Frank would never do that," she screamed. The conversation was cut off because as I warned her it would, the spaghetti came back up.

She had morning sickness all day long, and it did not stop after the first few months. When the conversation resumed, she continued to insist that Frank could not have done what I knew he did. She was caught up in her guilt and I had too much pride to roll over and accept what she had done. We left it there and went to sleep in our separate beds, two exhausted and troubled people.

The following day I found the missing piece in the Hoffman case. My good friend Steven knew already what was there, but he was in no position to tell me while he represented the Hoffmans. But there it was buried in one of the police forms from the night Mrs. Hoffman was treated at the hospital. One of the cops had examined Senator Hoffman's car. It was the car he used to bring his wife to the hospital. There was blood on the passenger side seat and floor. They felt free to inspect the vehicle because it was a state owned vehicle and no search warrant was needed. A dubious assumption, but I had no need of the cars contents.

The police after inspecting the vehicle made no arrest that night because Mrs. Hoffman stuck to her story of falling. But why did Hoffman have the state car? The answer was easily found. He had spent the early evening at a public meeting in Rochester, having driven there directly from a similar meeting in Syracuse. In fact he had been traveling all over Upstate New York selling his unpopular position on fracking for natural gas. I did the math and I knew. The Senator had in fact never been interviewed just accused. Neither had he defended himself.

OFFENCE AND JUSTICE

*****

Frank Patterson was sure that a car was following his. The vehicle was a rather non-descript late model sedan, and it was there and gone, but back again as he looked in his real view mirror. His Mercedes GT was not a hard car to follow through city traffic. He was worried. There had been rumors about an FBI investigation. He needed to be careful.

Since seducing Laura Parker, Frank's life had not been his usual carefree overindulgent existence. That husband of hers had proved to be something out of the ordinary. Usually the husbands had to suck it up when he bedded their wives. Frank was a well off partner in a powerful law firm. He was both good looking and the confident type women are attracted to. How could he be setup and extorted by a second rate ADA and his wimpy defense lawyer buddy? It was humiliating. When you considered that this happened in the backwater that is the Capital of New York where everyone knows everyone else, it was not acceptable. He had to retaliate.

How could he just let it go? He could see that pretty little cuckold Fitzgerald laughing at him because Sullivan got the best of him. Frank was born to be top dog. He was big physically, had gone to the best schools, had always been well off financially; but those two had taken his money and hurt his pride. Afterwards Saul Solomon had dressed him down like a school boy, and warned him to keep his pants zipped. Solomon told him to stay away from Sullivan. He said that prick was going places and was dangerous. What then was Frank, a second rate loser?

"You always drive this slow?" asked the attractive brunette in the Mercedes passenger seat.

The girl was not his usual type. He preferred them more upscale and married if possible. The waitress Trina, was good looking, but single with kids. He had met her formerly in a bar where she worked, and then recently in the little coffee shop around the corner from his office. At the bar, she had been cool toward him, but later from behind the coffee counter she was all smiles and come on. She was not in his class, but since he had been shut out of the office pussy pool by that prick Solomon, he had to take it where he could. She also knew how to party and where to find the goods.

"Just being careful- want to get us there in one piece," he said.

"It's just that I thought you would be more anxious," she said moving her hand up his thigh and giving a little giggle.

In spite of himself he sped up.

*****

"Mr. Rosencrantz, PLEASE ENOUGH!" Judge Thompson pleaded.

"But your Honor my client is being denied his constitutional rights," Attorney Matthew Rosencrantz said for about the tenth time. Matt wasn't a bad lawyer he simply had a bad case. He was a tall distinguished fifty something lawyer who had graduated Cornell law at the age of twenty-seven and proceeded into the family legal business. Where he had a modest career based on his unusual persistence and generally likable disposition. But he had worn-out Judge Thompson's patience.

"For the last time, if Mr. Sullivan is so misguided as to grant your client immunity from prosecution in this matter he cannot refuse to testify," His Honor said, then turned on me with invective.

"Don't think I won't report this matter to the proper authorities Mr. Sullivan. I'm not sure what dirty political deal has been made, but I for one am not going to keep silent." The Judge had a bit of a temper I thought, but then people say I do as well.

In the Grand Jury room, Senator Hoffman's attitude was equal parts fear and anger. The members of the jury did not view him with much sympathy. I had been taken aside by one of the Deputy Attorney Generals that had been working with this jury and given a briefing on its makeup.

"They're a little on the old side, not unusual. They've been sitting awhile and it's easier if they don't have pressing obligations. The foreperson is an Asian-Indian woman in her sixties, a naturalized citizen, very proud of that fact, serious about her obligations here. Apparently she read up on the Grand Jury procedure and knows she can ask questions. A bit difficult, if I had to do it over, I wouldn't pick her. The rest can be led if you need," she said.

The Deputy AG then gave me another up-and-down look and one of those come-on smiles I had been receiving from nearly every female on the AG staff. It had gotten so bad that Sid Levy took me aside and asked if I wanted him to take some action. I begged him not to since I was desperately trying to have my little staff treated well by his. I did not need any friction over some looks, a few suggestive remarks, and the occasional unnecessary physical contact.

He walked away shaking his head and saying, "Life was a bit simpler when all you needed to do was protect the females on the staff." His problem was that he had a sixty-forty split favoring female attorneys, with his good guy effort to be an equal opportunity employer in an era when more females are graduating law schools than males. Problem was they were attorneys and aggressive and they spent most of their adult lives studying to get ahead, now they were either looking for partners or some fun. A lot of his male staff was gay, some inherited from predecessors and other attracted by the good working conditions for gays. The result was a ratio of heterosexual males consistent with a night at a Broadway theater. The unattached males were few indeed. Great for the guys-unless you had a jealous, pregnant, and emotionally fragile estranged spouse.

As I walked into the jury room to do battle with Senator Hoffman; I was thinking that if it went well, I might-just might be able to get my own office space. When sworn in, the Senator immediate asserted spousal privilege.

"To what Senator?" I asked.

"To everything," he said. Out of the corner of my eye, I could see the Indian lady taking notes.

"You have to wait until I ask a question," I said trying to sound slightly amused. "Care to confer with your attorney on that."

"No," he said.

"Alright, when did you arrive home on March 25th, of this year?" I asked.

"I can't remember."

"You brought your wife to Mercy General at 9:46 pm.," I said showing him the admission record and the subsequent police report. "So it must have been before then."

He didn't respond so I went on.

"Witnesses say you left Rochester a little before 8 pm. CORRECT?"

"YES," he said reluctantly.

"Normally how long would it take you to get home?" I asked.

He knew where I was going and was reluctant to answer.

"Maybe forty-five minutes to an hour."

"The State Police assure me the trip would take an hour and ten minutes at least in good weather, but that night they had what is referred to as a lake effect storm in Rochester. Snow, CORRECT?"

"Yes," he said, but you could barely hear the word.

I leaned toward him. "Senator you had barely enough time to get home, find your wife in distress and get her to the hospital! If you didn't hit her, who did?" We were eye to eye as I said this.

Hoffman set his jaw and responded: "I evoke spousal privilege."

I pulled back, as I did I saw the Jury forewoman's hand shoot up.

I turned acknowledging her, "Can he do that?" she asked.

I turned back to Hoffman before I answered. "Maybe- it's a close point, what he knows has to have come from his wife, which she told him because he was her husband. But whether the privilege applies here is a close point. However, he is betting that I will try to force an answer and take long enough that he will be crucified in the press and the vultures will be satisfied with his head. But I won't."

Hoffman looked at me, the anger clear and apparent. "Damn you Sullivan," he said, then turned to face the jury.

"You don't know this man; he's not the young innocent he seems. He's, a political schemer of the worst kind. As a juvenile he nearly beat a priest to death. As a prosecutor he has shown that he'll do anything to win. He is a creature of our Governor and his political cronies. Please believe me I'm fighting to protect my family. You must have families, would you let them be destroyed so some politicians can pretend they believe in justice." He said this as the tears flowed down his cheeks to wet his dress shirt.

"Where was your son that night?" I said when he had stopped talking as if I'd heard nothing he'd said.

"What?"

"You heard me—Jerry junior. Your daughter Alice was in her dorm at NYU, they keep very accurate records of freshmen females. But where was your son?" I said moving closer to him again. "No privilege to invoke there."

"Goddamn you. Do you have no soul?"

"Senator by now you know, I know. The affair between your wife and the black Reverend and what it led to. -Do we need to call the witnesses to testify?" I said and then I turned to the jury.

I waved my hand broadly for effect at the jury, "these good people are intelligent, they understand that if you could not have committed the crime, then someone else did and that someone needed a similar motive," I said and could see the light bulb blinking on for the jurymen.

"So where was your son?"

Hoffman looked about crushed.

"I promised Elsa,(his wife)" he said.

"Just give us the truth there's nothing else for it now."

And with that he did. Mom had wanted her son with her when she gave the bad news about the pregnancy to Dad, but she hadn't counted on the son's reaction. Junior hit her one good hard blow; she was standing in the dining room at the time and fell the two steps into the sunken living room. She struck a small end table but appeared, except for a black eye, to have escaped injury.

OFFENCE AND JUSTICE

An hour later the miscarriage started by then the son had left angry, but having apologized profusely for the blow he struck. When Mr. Hoffman got home his wife was bleeding and experiencing cramps. He rushed her to the hospital about ten minutes from their home. What followed was the families attempt to conceal the crime and societies need to punish the abusive husband guilty or not.

I asked the jury for a statement that no charge could be brought against the Senator. They were more than willing, but:

"Can't we indict the son?" the forewoman asked, "Is that not our duty?"

"Sorry, but I don't have jurisdiction over him, he holds no elected office and my jurisdiction is limited to those that do," I said, not exactly the interpretation of my office some would give, but what I had decided I was going to hold to.

"However," I said seeming to ponder the question, "If you wish you may refer the matter to the local DA and the State Attorney General setting forth your reasons," which is what they did.

*****

The Albany Times Union covered it on Page four. It was not a big news item and something of an occurrence that was becoming more common. A prominent attorney found dead in his home. Drugs were suspected, another tragedy in the growing trend of prominent people succumbing to addiction.

CHAPTER EIGHT

The local police got there first, but soon seeded the scene to the state police. The FBI showed up but got the brush off. They were out of their jurisdiction and prominent people were concerned. Frank Patterson had more friends in death than he had in life. The investigation was quick and conclusive. Frank died of a heroin overdose; a very high quality of the drug had been apparently snorted or otherwise ingested.

When found Frank had been dead several days and his activities on the day of his death were vague. Those who had seen him early that evening thought he might have been with a dark haired woman, but no one knew her. Not one of his regular lady friends. At any rate nothing suggested others were involved. Franks alcohol abuse and his lifestyle suggested he may have fallen victim to experimenting with a drug he was not familiar with. The State Police report was accidental overdose, but many were doubtful. However, all they had were doubts.

*****

The release of the Grand Jury verdict had to be done with care. I wanted as little publicity as possible. Fridays are busy news days by releasing late Thursday we missed that cycle and hopefully headed into a cycle where the news from upstate New York would get buried. Well, it was an idea.

Thursday at four forty-five we issued the decision. At five thirty Kat came into my office.

"Thought you went home," I said.

"The lobby is filled with reporters and camera crews looking for you," she said.

I gave a frustrated sigh knowing there was no escape only delay.

"Ok, issue a statement that there will be a press conference tomorrow at Noon as I sneak out through the garage," I said hoping that this would become unimportant by the following day.

I managed to get home without incident only to find the press on my lawn waiting. There weren't that many, the cable news and two local newspapers. As I hobbled on my crutches toward my front door I put them off pleading the news conference the following day. But they surprised me asking that I comment on the statement by Steven Fitzgerald.

"And what did Mr. Fitzgerald have to say?" I asked.

The girl from the cable news stuck a microphone in my face as she said: "Foxy says you can't make a case, so you are side-stepping the issue."

I laughed, "Well maybe he thinks he can do better," I said as I ducked into my house leaving them with something but not much. Steven was only doing his job kicking the ball back to my end of the field.

I knew something was wrong when I entered the house. It was dark and silent although Laura's Mercedes was parked in the driveway.

She was in the back bedroom where she had been sleeping. We had not been sharing a bed. At first, this was purely my physical and emotional condition but later it was partly hers. She was not sleeping well. They say some women glow when they are pregnant, not Laura. She got much bigger in the belly, but smaller almost everywhere else. Her face was thin and drawn with dark circles under her eyes. She had seemed to be in a general decline.

In truth, I had not been much of a husband or future father. I had let my pride and anger loose on her without regard for the consequences. Lately, involved with the problems of the special counsel office, I had been indifferent to her. Now she was lying on the bed fully clothed, her breathing labored and her skin tone a sickly gray. I tried to wake her but she was unresponsive. I called 911.

SIR PATRICK BIJOU

The ambulance arrived with the cable news still hanging about. Apparently, they monitor the emergency broadcasts. They filmed the whole scene of the paramedics arriving followed by the ambulance. We took Laura to the hospital. We arrived and I was scuttled to a waiting room where I could watch what just happened on the TV.

Two hours later I met with Laura's OBGYN, a late fifties woman with gray hair pulled back into a bun. She was about five foot four worth of pissed off.

"What about being a husband and father don't you understand Mr. Sullivan?"

"Look things are a little strained in our marriage right now."

"Oh, so when I've been telling you for months that your wife needed to work less and eat more, you never heard me? And you are blind as well as deaf. Did you even notice whether she was eating or taking the vitamins and supplements I was prescribing?" she asked giving me that look women reserve for idiots.

"We haven't been eating much together since she set the kitchen ablaze. I tried a few times, but she didn't seem to keep her food down," I said realizing that I had left a woman who can't cook on her own most of the time.

She shook her head. "YOUR WIFE is dehydrated, emaciated, and anemic and that's just her. The baby I fear will be low birth weight with all the complications that involves. Now I suggest that you pull yourself together and start acting like a husband and a soon to be father." With that said, she left me to ponder my short comings.

They let me into Laura's room, she still wasn't awake. A kindly nurse assured me she was stable and would be all right. I hunkered down in a rather uncomfortable chair and waited. We were in the ICU for the night. I was told my being allowed to stay was a privilege they were granting me due to the situation. Between the bouts of guilt and the uncomfortable chair I did not get much sleep. Early the next morning Laura was awake, and they were getting ready to move her to another room. They were serving her breakfast and it was not optional. I stayed to make sure she ate.

I wanted to speak to her but before I could in breezed Susan Singleton.

"Laura what going on, you're all over the news?" Susan said.

Laura looked guilty and embarrassed, "I had a bad spell yesterday, worked too hard I guess," she said in a weak voice.
"Well get ready for some company. The Governor's coming to see you," Susan gushed.

The Hospital staff was excited. The Governor was making his visit with the media in tow. Laura was placed in a private room. She was made as presentable as possible. Security showed up and everyone was turned out from hospital administrators to Laura doctor who looked a bit tired.

Edward Kincade came into the room alone, shooing Susan out as he did. He shook my hand and patted me on the shoulder.

"Damn good job on the Hoffman case Pat, knew I picked you for a reason," The Governor said then turned to Laura.

"You gave us a scared young woman, but your doctor assures me you are going to be all right. We having a boy or a girl?" he asked.

"A girl, Governor," she said.

"Hey just Ed or Gov if you must, when we're alone. Now I'm glad you're feeling better, but I must steal your husband for a few minutes. I will send him back soon with orders to stay with you until you are better." Then he dragged me into the corner.

"What do I need to know about the Hoffman situation?" he asked. So I gave him a brief run down.

"Shit, who else knows this?"

"My investigator Phil Sloan and of course the hospital staff who treated Ms. Hoffman," I said.

"Ok now keep a lid on it while I try to save Hoffman's career. But now you and I need to go out and take a bow and assure the public that everything is just fine with everyone, especially Laura here. That's right everything is fine with your wife, no stupid problems with things that are over, done and best forgotten," he said with a nonnegotiable look.

I nodded as once again I realized I had maneuvered myself to a place I did not want to be.

The press conference that followed was brief and to the point. Jerry Hoffman was a good man wrongly accused. The people of the state owed a debt of gratitude to the hard working special prosecutor who had sacrificed much to see justice done. I took my bow and then was plummeted with questions about my wife's health. Laura had upstaged the indictment. But it was not all clear sailing; the reporter from the Rochester Gazette was not being distracted. He asked about Jerry Jr. and why he was not indicted. I gave my prepared answer about Jurisdiction. At that moment Susan stepped in.

"I believe we need to let the Special Prosecutor go back to his wife now," she said and with that broke up the press conference.

At that point I was allowed to go back to my wife's room. Laura was asleep. Around noon Kat called and I dictated a formal statement on the indictment which said nothing. She went down and read it to the assembled reports with my regrets that I was unavailable due to a family emergency. The reporters wanted updates on Laura's condition. Kat told them she was well and sleeping.

The nurse woke Laura at 12:45 for lunch. It was time to talk.

"What do you think you're doing Laura?" I began.

"I'm sorry, I made more trouble, but I didn't mean to."

"Why haven't you been eating?"

"I get sick."

"You could have told me you were having serious problems."

"I couldn't, what was I going to say, I failed as a wife and now I'm going to fail as a mother."

"You're not going to fail as a mother. We'll work on your diet and fatten you up, keep you home and rested. Solomon can get along without you for a while."

"I wish it were that simple," she said "I'm no good at this. I tried, believe me, I tried."

"So now we will try," I said.

"You don't mean that."

"Don't tell me what I mean. For now we're in this together. Live with it," I said.

She broke down crying. I wasn't sure why. The nurse came in and told me to leave for a bit.

I spent the next three days in and around the Hospital before they sent her home. The rest of the world was not standing still. Reporters were calling my office trying to find out anything. They were also sneaking around the Hospital. The doctor confronted me on the third day.

"I'm going to release your wife to go home. That means home not work. I also want someone with her at all times for the present. She is stable and we need to keep her that way. I have a visiting nurse set up to help her. I recommend you get a home health aide." She was giving me a look like she expected a fight.

"I'm not the problem here. Laura seems to be having problems accepting help. Seems to think it is some kind of failure on her part," I said.

"She is depressed. I believe it's your marital situation. If I were you I'd put on a happy face, if not for her think of the baby," she said then she reached out and grasped my shoulder. "Marriage is never easy- being a parent is harder. Sometimes you have to do what your family needs not what you want. It's time to grow up."

I would have argued, but she was right. Don my therapist gave me some good leads on home health workers and a nice fortyish mother of three was hired to help. She was a cheerful woman who meshed well with Laura and was very supportive. She had lots of tricks to keep the food down and the expectant mother's spirits up.

Things were looking up until we got the phone call. Kat fielded it first then in went to Mary Ellen, but he was not being put off and he wanted to speak to the boss.

"This is Jack Rubins from the Rochester—"he began, but I cut him off.

"I know who you are Mr. Rubins and where you're from, as my staff said we have no comment."

"I still have to ask," he said.

"Then go ahead."

"You obviously know about Elsa Hoffman's extra marital affair and the miscarriage. So how and when did you learn those facts?" I could hear the smug satisfaction in his voice. He had done his job, now he wanted to reap the maximum return.

"The question is how did you learn those facts Mr. Rubin. I can only think that you bribed some person or persons, possibly public officials," I said.

"My sources are confidential," he said.

"Yes, but I would much rather prosecute you," I said hoping to run this bluff.

"Your crazy how can you do that?"

"Poorly written statute doesn't say what I can or can't do."

"Yes and I know you must have done something illegal to get your information," he said.

"Pity there's no one charged with prosecuting me," I said.

"Ok I get it- want to make a statement or not?"

"If I see a fair article that tries not to be too scandalous, I won't ask how you got your information and I'll send you a copy of my report to the legislature the day I file it," I said.

"You're going to file a report on the Hoffman case," he asked

"No, just a quarterly report that outlines our activities and what my staff discovered on any matter investigated," I said.

"When can I expect to see this report?" he asked.

"Well this is Wednesday next Tuesday I should think."

Several days later Jack Rubin broke the story in the Rochester Gazette. He was very fair. He gave the history of the Hoffman's long marriage and described Elsa's major injury as unintended. But he laid it out including his belief that my office had discovered most of this information, although that was stated to be speculation.

The New York City tabloids were not near as kind. They opened with pictures side by side of Mrs. Hoffman and her lover.

I had given Mary Ellen the job of writing our version. She did a great job, Phil came out looking like Sherlock Homes and I like a remarkably skilled prosecutor who gambled and won. Our version said nothing about a miscarriage which we believed; "was not supported by the facts." The affair was fairly certain based on the witnesses at the correctional facility, but Senator Hoffman's innocence was beyond doubt due to his travel that evening.

"Hello MACHER," Saul Solomon said when I picked up the phone. "You know what that means?" he asked.

"Yiddish for big shot," I said.

"Ten million big, you got funded. The Dems wanted to give you five but the opposition wanted to make sure you would be happy, so they amended it up and gave you the same salary as the Governor." He said.

"Thank you," I said and meant it.

"My pleasure, but you did well; you'll be a politician yet."

"Have you seen the Times today?" Saul asked.

"No, I try not to read the City papers."

"Read the Editorial Macher," he said then hung up.

New York Times July 8, 2014.

THE GOVERNOR CHOSE WELL

Many, ourselves included, wondered if Governor Edward Kincade's choice for what amounted to a Corruption CZAR was up to the task. Patrick X. Sullivan, the little known former VanPatten County prosecutor was both young and inexperienced. What recognition he had earned was for courage in standing up to a vicious drug gang. He is a direct sort of young man who was not known for his legal or political skills. His close ties to the Governor, his mentor, were also troubling in an office that clearly needed an independent person.

The doubters have been proven wrong; with skill and a gambler's daring, the young prosecutor has proven himself more than worthy of his office. He has resolved a difficult and troubling incident and restored the reputation of a respected public official. Sullivan had done so in spite of a physical limitation and at some considerable personal cost. Now it is up to the legislature.

Fund the office you created now that it is occupied by the proper person.

In reality, I had one last problem. She was past seven months pregnant, doing physically better, but still not out of the woods. What amazed me was how I had misjudged her. She had seemed this confident even dynamic person, always in control, able to climb the rickety latter of the corporate law firm. She was the classic over-achiever. How could I know that it was all a front, that beneath the surface she was this insecure girl?

What I had taken for strength was weakness. She wasn't reaching for me as an equal; I was the buttress she was trying to lean on. She was weak and I was strong, and she had expected me to support her no matter what she did. Manipulating me was part of the game. She could not win fair, she had to cheat. But it was different from Steven, who cheated for the fun of it, or I who cheated to win. My beautiful and sexy wife cheated to survive.

Laura's current problem was that there was no cheating the little person inside her who was getting ready to come out. The closer the time came the greater her fear grew. She had the names picked out, Bridget for my mother and Ellen for hers. Little Bridget E Sullivan was awaited by both our family's with anticipation.

*****

I was rocking on the odd slide-swing set that Laura and Don had set up on the back patio. It was a comfortable seat. Bridget was in my arms, her mother was hovering nearby. My daughter had ten little fingers and toes and they were all wrapped firmly around my heart. I started loving her when she came bloody from her mother's womb, all six pounds two ounces of her. She had a little dark hair then now six weeks later it was a few white hairs. My mother said she would be a red head, "That's how you started all colorless."

The families that had descended on us after the birth had gone home, now we were alone except for the hired help. Laura was proving to be super mom, the over-achiever had settled in again. She had given birth without a whimper and was out of the hospital the same day, against the doctor's wishes. She had already informed me or was it warned me she would no longer be using birth control.

"If you stay with me this is going to be a traditional marriage. I'll work only part-time because I'm still no good at being a housewife, but I will be barefoot in the kitchen and pregnant most of the time," she said.

"Absolutely not," I replied.

"Pat please I want to do this."

"Laura barefoot ok, pregnant maybe if you behave, but kitchen never, it's strictly off limits." I said.

She laughed. "Ok, just barefoot and pregnant." Then hugging me she asked:

SIR PATRICK BIJOU

"Am I forgiven?"

"No, but I love you and my daughter so I'll stick around, besides your good for the image."

Indeed she was, she got excellent press coverage for the birth. Yes I did forgive her but I would never tell her that. As to worrying about her future fidelity, well the rumors still keep going around about what happened to poor Frank. I think most people make some assumptions. A man would need a lot of courage to fool with Mrs. Sullivan, which is what people call my wife these days.

I handed Bridget to her mother.

"I have to go they're waiting for me," I said.

She nodded and gave me a wan smile, "Please don't be long, I miss you when you're gone."

"I won't be long, I just need to meet some politicians."

She did not say what she was thinking, which was that a politician was exactly what I had become. Odd when you feel about it, I do not seem well suited to the profession. I have to struggle with it every day. But as I left, I took a long look at my wife sitting with our baby in her arm. Laura had a broad smile and I realized that I never had really seen her this happy or relaxed. All her fears were fading. This was my family and I would protect it.

*****

EPILOGUE

The service was held in a Troy in little church near the Hudson. It was a relatively new Church by Troy standards dating from the middle of the nineteenth century. A stone building composed of Manhattan Sand Stone normally referred to as brown stone. The stones were set well. They showed wear, but not deterioration. Small grooves showed along the foundation where the Hudson had flooded over the centuries.

The memorial service had been well planned by a junior associate of the firm. Frank Patterson had been officially listed as a Methodist, but the Church was one of Tory's Episcopal houses of worship with their tiffany stained glass windows and tolerant attitudes. Death by drug overdose was of no concern. The fact that the deceased and few of the attendees were of the Episcopal faith made the service no different than the average Sunday service since few of the attendees at any service were Episcopalian. Being Christian was nice, but not required.

The black priest who oversaw the service was not remotely familiar with the decedent, but he did a remarkable job of invoking the proper spirit of the one year anniversary of the death. Saul Solomon was well pleased with the turn out and the service that he had determined was the proper tribute to a fallen member of the firm. All went remarkable well; several of the staff spoke in tribute to Frank including Saul who left none in doubt that he saw this death as a tragic accident. He had already made clear he would tolerate no spreading of rumors otherwise in the office or out.

Saul left the Church last passing under Tiffany's vision of the kingdom of heaven in stained glass at the back of the Church. Laura had not been present, having been sent to San Francisco on important firm business thus avoiding the awkward possibility of her husband being at the service. However, as Saul passed through the Church vestibule or narthex shaking the Priests hand and thanking him, he caught sight of Steven Fitzgerald standing on the Church steps.

"Good afternoon Mr. Fitzgerald how good of you to come, but I'm somewhat surprised considering," Saul said.

"The man was a client, if only briefly, Mr. Solomon—and please Foxy will do," Steven replied breaking into a small smile as if laughing at himself.

"Well then you must call me Sal," Solomon replied.

"Sal it is then. I'm just waiting for my wife she's picking me up," Fitzgerald said.

"Yes my wife Martha's gone to get our Lincoln," Saul said.

"Ah much more practical than a Mercedes sport's car, but you know my wife Susan I believe?" Steve replied.

"Yes, a most beautiful woman. You are very fortunate," Saul said.

"Yes, on these occasions one must appreciate one's blessings."

Saul though a moment then decided he had to ask, even though he was sure he would receive no answer. "Some still believe that Frank met with foul play—what's your opinion?" he asked.

Steven reflected a moment then spoke very seriously. "Well I see Frank's actions as a series of unfortunate miscalculations that led to a tragic result. Every action has a consequence. It's troubling how these consequences are not always foreseeable," Steven said.

"But surely when you take on much stronger opponents losing must be predictable."

"Spoken as a man of perception who has had to navigate the rocky shoals of life. A good Jewish boy from Brooklyn who has used his brains to rise in the world and obtain the good life with his Goya wife," Steven was virtually smirking as he said this.

"So he underestimated you Foxy. For it was the act of a fox not a wolf," Saul replied letting what he suspected out.

Steven smiled, "A guess without evidence."

"Tell me did the wolf arrive before or after that priest raped you?" Saul said, some of the rage he felt overtaking him. If Steven Fitzgerald was upset he did not show it.

"Sort of in between," he replied then continued, "You should have seen his face. He'd picked a location where no one could hear my screams, but Pat is the protective sort. Of course once that temper of his is truly lost he goes from merely dangerous to deadly. Lucky someone heard the priest's cries," Steven said without emotion.

"I would say Foxy you're just as deadly when you want to be," Saul said.

"A fox must live by his wits not his passions. Only what is necessary. As I said actions have consequences—but my ride has arrived," he said taking his leave.

Saul watched the late model Mercedes sport coupe pull away from the curb to be replaced by his wife's Lincoln Towncar. He walked wearily to the passenger door. As he seated himself in the car Martha turned to him.

"Something wrong Sal, you don't look well?" she said.

"I'm fine, just been trying to purge my sins," he said still feeling guilty about what had happened to the foolish Frank Patterson. You should be very careful before you touch a man like Sullivan's wife. If you get away in one piece you should count yourself lucky. To strike back was suicidal. If it hadn't been Fitzgerald, it would have been someone else. Still, Saul felt that guilt.

Martha looked over at her husband: "Well it was a very fine service you should be proud. Too bad Laura and that nice husband of hers were not here," she said and Saul smiled at his wife.

The End

ABOUT THE AUTHOR

Sir Patrick Bijou writesfor the sexual liberation of all people, focusing on the beautiful people who are often left out of sexual stories and images, including queer people, trans people, and people of color whose everyday lives include the thrill of **LOVING.**

Thank you again for purchasing this book, I hope you have enjoyed it!

AUTHOR SIR PATRICK BIJOU.

www.ingramcontent.com/pod-product-compliance
Lightning Source LLC
Chambersburg PA
CBHW071609080526
44588CB00010B/1073